Ghosts:

Minnesota's Other
Natural Resource

Brian Leffler

4880 Lower Valley Road Atglen, Pennsylvania 19310

Published by Schiffer Publishing Ltd.
4880 Lower Valley Road
Atglen, PA 19310
Phone: (610) 593-1777; Fax: (610) 593-2002
E-mail: Info@schifferbooks.com

For the largest selection of fine reference books on this and related subjects, please
visit our web site atWe are always looking for people to write books on new and related subjects. If you have an idea for a book please contact us at the above address.

This book may be purchased from the publisher.
Include $3.95 for shipping.
Please try your bookstore first.
You may write for a free catalog.

In Europe, Schiffer books are distributed by
Bushwood Books
6 Marksbury Ave.
Kew Gardens
Surrey TW9 4JF England
Phone: 44 (0) 20 8392-8585; Fax: 44 (0) 20 8392-9876
E-mail: info@bushwoodbooks.co.uk
Website: www.bushwoodbooks.co.uk
Free postage in the U.K., Europe; air mail at cost.

Back Cover:
This is an ectoplasm that was captured at the Lakeview Cemetery in Buhl, Minnesota.
It is a prime example of just how ectoplasm shows up in photography. *Photo taken by Brian Leffler*

Designed by Mark David Bowyer
Type set in Batik Regular / NewBaskerville BT

ISBN: 978-0-7643-2713-1
Printed in China

Contents

Acknowledgments

I would very much like to thank the St. Louis County Historical Society for their contribution of information about the Hibbing area.

I would very much like to thank the Cass County Historical Society for their contribution of information about the Chase on the Lake Hotel.

I would very much like to thank all of the wonderful people from the Duluth Omni Max Theater and the *William A. Irvin* for their invaluable information on this wonderful ship.

I would very much like to thank Ken Buhler at the Duluth Depot for all of the wonderful experiences and information about this great place.

Finally, I would like to thank Jane Ranum for providing me with such a fantastically detailed history on her family and home in Grand Marais.

Dedication

This book is dedicated first of all to my mom, Linda. She is the person that believed I could do whatever I wanted to do. Although much of my life has seemed to be a disappointment to her, as well as heartache, she has stood by me and welcomed all of my lifelong decisions. She has been a lifetime support system for me which has meant that through my earlier mistakes in life, she has given up many good years helping me battle many of life's hard knocks that we all experience in one form or another. She wanted to be a writer of fiction at one point in her life, but never got the chance to have her work published. Mom, you can take pride in knowing that you have very much helped me get to where I am today and have been a major factor in this book ever being written.

Secondly, this book is dedicated to my wife, Rhonda, who has been a major factor for this book being written also. She has supported me and allowed me to take the time I needed to get the words written down. She has been supportive on those very busy Halloween holidays when it has been one interview or radio show or television news cast after another until the day finally culminates in an investigation somewhere, usually with outside people tagging along for the ride because they won a radio contest.

Thirdly, my kids, John and Jeff, have been a helping factor by keeping me going from day to day. What I do, I do for them. They are two kids who have already had a lot of adversity in their young lives. It has been devastating for them, but they have proven resilient enough to pick themselves up and move forward.

I only hope that I have proven myself to my family—that I am as good a dad, husband, and son as they'd wish for me to be.

Last but not least, I want very much to thank the wonderful group of people that are the Northern Minnesota Paranormal Investigators. This group has shown professionalism in all that we do as a group. They represent us every day with pride and do a wonderful job dealing with the clients who we have worked with over the years. They also give up family time and other, important things that they need to do in order to participate in these investigations and evidence review. They even go as far as giving up work shifts to other co-workers in order to attend a function with the group. That shows true dedication to our cause when members are willing to give up some of the family livelihood in order to go someplace and help someone else out with their situation—something that they don't understand or feel the least bit comfortable with. I want to list each individually here so that you can get to know them before reading the following pages, as well as a thank you to each one so that they know how much I really appreciate each and every one of them—I don't always say it as I should.

Phil Bodle. Phil has been in the group longer than anyone with the exception of myself. He has done a wonderful job for the group on many investigations, and since he is such a big, strong young man, he ends up being our mule half the time by carrying loads of equipment. Thank you, Phil.

Rhonda Leffler. (Well, you already know how I feel here.) Rhonda has brought a lot of stability and reason to the team that we definitely need all the time. There are times when others make mistakes and she comes shining through as the voice of reason.

She also brings a psychic element to the team that has been a very valuable tool for us. Thank you, Rhonda.

Christy Sandnas. Christy is next in line by seniority. She has been a psychic leader of the team for years now and even though I have been amazed over and over with the information she gets psychically on a constant basis, I have grown to trust her insights implicitly. Thank you, Christy.

Kyle Bruzenak. Kyle has been on the team since Halloween of 2005. He won a radio contest locally and was able to come along with the team during that promotional investigation. He impressed the team so much that he was immediately asked to join and has done a wonderful job with the team ever since. Kyle is also the tech specialist of the group, always figuring new ways to chase ghosts and set up equipment. Thank you, Kyle.

Gina Hill. Gina joined the group immediately after Kyle. Her first investigation was the one at Moon Lake. Gina is always one to sacrifice for the group and comes through with whatever is needed. She volunteers to drive and shuttle people around, as well as being a solid investigator for the team. She is also very good at sifting through the evidence. Thank you, Gina.

Tiffany Latvala. Tiffany is our newest member of the team. She joined us in the summer of 2006. I must say that she has been very impressive to all of us by being at everything she can possibly attend, even at a moments notice, if at all possible. She is also proving to be a very solid investigator and is also coming along wonderfully with the evidence. Thank you, Tiffany.

A Note From the Author

Ghosts: Minnesota's Other Natural Resource is a journey through some of the best haunts in Minnesota. The haunted locations included inside these pages are places that you have not read about a dozen times before. The encounters and paranormal experiences are first-hand, not rumors or just stories, but the actual encounters told by the people who have lived them and are still living them today.

Several places explored in this book are open to the public and invite anyone who is willing to have an encounter of their own to join them in the experience. Many others are the ordeals of private families who really want to share their experiences in the hope that they will eventually help other people to understand and better deal with their own paranormal experiences—should they encounter something that goes bump in the night.

Throughout these pages you will also find some interesting investigation tips, which come from an investigator who has researched ghosts and hauntings for over ten years. I hope that you will join the best investigative team in the state of Minnesota for a journey through some of the best hauntings that they have ever dealt with.

Introduction
Iron Ore, Timber, and the Ghosts of Many Hard Workers

It all began on May 11, 1858, when Minnesota was adopted into the United States of America as it's thirty-second state. That year, Henry Sibley was named as the first governor of this great state. Minnesota becoming a state and all of the pomp and circumstance soon gave way to what gave this state its real heart. It has had a strong heart beat over these many years, due to the fact that it was born of the sweat and blood of the residents who have made a life here.

Team N.M.P.I. Taken at the *U. S. S. William A. Irvin*, Duluth, Minnesota. Front row from left to right: Gina Hill, Tiffany Latvals, Kyle Bruzenak, and Phil Bodle. Back row from left to right: Christy Sandnas, Rhonda Leffler, and Brian Leffler. *Photo courtesy of Laurie Bruzenak*

Sure, this was a struggle most of the time for the residents of this new state, but that didn't seem to matter. They took the bull by the horns so-to-speak and met every challenge head on. Most of the settlers here in the early days were immigrants from Germany, Finland, and Sweden and made up the largest portion of the settler's population. They were the ones who built the buildings, harvested the wheat in the summer, and the trees in the winter. They were the heart and soul of Minnesota, and as a paranormal investigator; I have seen this heart and soul in many places across our state.

There are really two industries that put Minnesota on the map; timber and iron mining. Timber began almost as a sideline venture. It was something that was much easier to do in the winter. Most of the timber men worked all spring, summer, and fall as farmers, moving to the timber industry to keep the cash flow coming in during those hard, cold Minnesota winter months. With the ground frozen, they could get their horses and men back into the swampy lands where travel was impossible during the summer.

The logs were also much easier to move across snow and ice which made their work so much more efficient. This business was a very tough one, however, even though they had log movement and travel down to an art form—this is Minnesota, and it gets well below zero for long stretches in the winter. These very rough conditions during the winter made the timber industry a very dangerous proposition at best. There were many men who froze to death, contracted diseases with no known cure, and got many infections and frostbite.

The mining industry was just as dangerous, if not more. There was still the risk of freezing to death and frostbite in the winter, but this industry was dangerous even in the summer. Many people got caught in cave-ins or fell to their deaths. There was also very large and dangerous machinery to watch out for, and sometimes, the worst would happen. Both industries became the building blocks on which a great state was built. These industries flourished and so did the men who worked the jobs, and more men were needed all the time to keep the industries growing. This influx of workers, most of which were immigrants at the time, needed places to live and start families. Towns were built, stores were opened, and schools were built for their children. So you can see just how important these industries were to the initial growth of Minnesota. Without these immigrants working and dying in the mines and in the woods, we would not be where we are today.

I am not a person who believes in order for a ghost to exist, there must be a tragic or sudden, violent death. I believe that a ghost can and does exist just upon the death of our bodies. A body is just a shell, in my opinion. It is our spirit that makes us who we truly are in the end. This spirit is what defines our personality as good or bad, honest or dishonest, friendly, or just plain mean. This spirit is what passes on to another plane of existence upon the death of our physical bodies. We will be the same in death as we were in life, since that spirit that makes us who we are is actually what passes on to the other side. This, I believe, is where people have described good and bad entities over the centuries.

Of course, there are good and bad entities since there are good and bad people in general. I believe that love is just as strong of an emotion as hatred, perhaps even stronger. This love could very well be a strong reason for a ghost to come back into our world to visit an object or us. It is pretty commonly agreed upon between people in the paranormal field of study that ghosts can attach themselves to both inanimate objects, as well as people themselves, and this has been encountered many times by my group, the Northern Minnesota Paranormal Investigators (and myself).

I once had a lady call me to ask me about a ghost problem in her home. She truly sounded upset that this was happening to her. Her home had never had any ghostly problems before that she was ever aware of, and it took me a few minutes to determine what her problem was. You see, she loved antiques and had purchased an old manual sewing machine in a very nice wooden cabinet. When she placed it at the end of the hall with a doily on it, she began to notice strange things happening in her home that she had never witnessed before.

After speaking with her for about half an hour or so, I learned of this purchase and told her to get it out of the house. She removed it promptly and her ghostly problems ceased. I believe that there was probably some woman who really loved her sewing machine, and her spirit has clung to that object even though the body died. This machine was probably a large part of her survival during her life and she had a very strong bond with this object for that reason.

I have also known people who have seen relatives. They have stated that they have seen their long lost great grandparents, for example. I firmly believe that these spirits hang around and keep an eye out for us. They are the ones who people refer to as "guardian angels." These long lost relatives try to help us at times, to keep us from harm's way. They are protectors and sometimes are that voice we all hear over our shoulders telling us that what we are about to do is not necessarily the right thing to do.

Many paranormal investigators have thought over the years that there are numerous different types or classifications of ghosts. I don't buy into it one bit. I think that a ghost is made up of electromagnetic energy and they use that to determine how they will appear to us. The only other term that I use is *poltergeist,* but that term describes the *type of haunting* as opposed to describing the *type of ghost* involved. Because *poltergeist* literally means "noise ghost" in German, when we have things like constant loud banging, audible voices, things being thrown around, and things missing only to be found later in the exact spot you checked ten times, we consider it to be a poltergeist haunting.

We have seen a major influx of "ghost hunters" over the past several years. This has been both a blessing as well as a curse for those of us who are more serious paranormal investigators. It has allowed us to write books of this nature, produce television shows, movies, and innumerable amounts of websites dedicated to the paranormal. This aspect of it is a definitive blessing for sure, but with this influx of people running around in supposedly haunted places, it has caused some access to be shut down.

Over the past several years, due to the massive influx of people entering the field, we have seen a great many people doing so without the proper amount of study or experience. This opens up the potential for having evidence that has not been properly scrutinized before its release, placed before the hard-nosed skeptics. This is not done intentionally, but happens primarily through lack of knowledge and experience.

Here are some things you should remember for the capture of paranormal evidence with a still camera:

- Use a 35 mm film camera with auto advance. This is the best method to use as it provides you with a negative that can be scrutinized by a professional and it can be verified that what is in the photograph, is actually something that was in front of the camera when the shot was taken.
- Do not use a digital camera. I do realize that they are easier and cheaper in the long-run, but they don't provide the investigator with any tangible evidence of the paranormal. They actually build the photograph for you and don't provide you with an actual true "snap" of what was in front of the camera. Through this building of the picture, it actually becomes manipulated evidence. Even the most expensive digital camera can drop pixels and cause anomalies that are not really in front of the camera.
- Digital camera photography is not admissible in a court of law in the United States. They are much too easily manipulated and thus don't make for sound evidence that is believable by the courts.
- Take the time to learn about mundane things, such as how dust and pollen appear on film, how motion blur affects a photograph, etc. Make sure that you conduct your own personal experiments to see just how things look on film before you ever head out to the field. This will very much help you to be able to better scrutinize your work, before it gets presented to the public.
- When developing your film, have the developer put only your photographs on a disk and not to actually print every shot. This will save you a tremendous amount of money in the end and make the use of film more appealing. Also, if at all possible, tell them not to cut your negative; but instead, keep it in whole and replace it back into the small plastic storage container. This will prevent any bad cuts that happen to chop into the negative of a great shot.

Here are some things you should remember for the capture of EVP (Electronic Voice Phenomena) on an investigation:

- Again, stick with analog equipment. For the same reasons as photography, you want very much to use standard magnetic recording tape.
- Make sure that you use a brand new tape at every recording session, and never re-use a tape. This can cause an issue with archival noise which can give a false positive result.
- Make sure that you never use the second side of the tape; this can give a false positive result due to bleed through on the tape. You think you have an EVP, but it is a voice of someone living that was recorded on the other side of the tape bleeding through to the side you are listening to.
- Digitals have an issue with archival noise that cannot be prevented. It can happen any time where something remains behind, providing yet another false positive result.
- Digitals should also be avoided since they will not provide any tangible evidence that can be scruitinized by a professional as an audio tape can be. Any evidence can easily be manipulated with these devices and the results cannot be verified in any way.

Another problem that has been caused by the massive influx of people into the paranormal field, is that there are people who are actually breaking into places and trespassing to try to collect paranormal evidence. Of course, most all of us will not condone the breaking of the law for any reason. Those people who do trespass in order to collect evidence, are causing problems for the rest of us, who are trying honestly to gather evidence and remain professional and upstanding.

- Never go onto someone else's property to investigate without their knowledge and permission. If you just ask, and they know that you are not going to trash the area, then most will not have a problem with you being there.

- Remember to police yourselves on other's property by cleaning up after yourselves and having a very high respect for property and owner while there. This will give them a good feeling about you and your group, which means that you very well may be able to make return trips to the location.

- Remember to do a walk-through in the light prior to attempting to move around in the pitch dark. An investigation can be very dangerous if you don't know what things you should be watching out for, such as holes in a floor or roots of trees sticking out of the ground. The last think anyone wants to have happen is for a medical emergency to ruin a good paranormal investigation.

I do realize that not everyone will agree with all of my thoughts and methods on the paranormal, but that is to be expected. Many of you will have your own methods of evidence collection, and that is all right, too. These are the methods used by both me and N.M.P.I. We have used them for many years and they have been tried and true for us. You won't go wrong if you follow these simple steps. I certainly hope that whether you agree with me or not, that you find this book to be an interesting journey through some extremely interesting paranormal locations in Northern Minnesota.

Chapter One
Lakeview Cemetery

Lakeview Cemetery in Buhl is a fantastic journey through paranormal experiences. There have been many accounts of things that have happened on those grounds in addition to the paranormal evidence collected through our investigations. It is a place that people have left abruptly as well as a place that some are afraid to go to visit loved ones who are buried there. Apparitions have been seen by several people and shadows have been seen darting from stone to stone, following people in the cemetery. Strange smells and inexplicable sounds that should not be there have also been reported.

"Sanctuary" photograph from Lakeview Cemetery. This is the area of the cemetery that we believe is not an active area for ghosts. *Photo taken by Brian Leffler*

The Shaw Hospital was the largest employer, aside from the iron mining industry, in the Buhl area just after the turn of the twentieth century. The Shaw Hospital was a sanatorium—the place that society sent the people it didn't want at the time. Sometimes this was for very good reason. Most of the people were laden with tuberculosis. There were also many there with various types of mental illness, mental retardation, and deformations. It was not a pleasant place to be, but necessary at the time.

In 1913, they began burying patients in Lakeview Cemetery when they died at the hospital. The problem was that most of them didn't have any money or family that cared about them in the least. This created a problem for the Shaw Hospital; they needed to do something to get rid of the bodies. Potter's Field was born. The graves were lined up in neat little rows, very close together, and were marked quite simply with an aluminum cross that had a number embossed on it. There are several hundred of these crosses out there.

It was a very different story for the patients who had money and family, of course. They got a burial with a good headstone and the recognition that they deserved with their names and dates of birth and death shown on it. In my opinion, it is this segregation and lack of recognition that has caused so much activity in this simple, unassuming cemetery.

The year 2003 seems to have been a banner year for paranormal evidence in the cemetery. We captured several things, including a fantastic video and EVP that will make the hair on the back of your neck stand straight up. I was walking through the oldest part of the cemetery in June of that year, talking to the spirits and attempting to collect some EVP. I was also carrying the camcorder—set on the night shots mode.

I had asked the spirits to "show us a sign" if any were about. Unbeknownst to me at the time, they did just that. I'd recorded an EVP on my tape recorder that was actually two different ghosts having a little bit of a conversation. The first voice said in a very gravelly voice, "There's no harm in that." The second voice immediately replied to the first saying, "Yeah, show 'em the flags, Roy."

I walked with the camcorder for about a minute when I noticed that a small flag—you know, the ones that go out on Memorial Day—was waving in the breeze. No big deal seeing flags waving, right? The only problem was that this time, there was no breeze to wave the flag. It was a very still night here in northern Minnesota, and that means one thing—bugs, bugs, and even more bugs! Of course, if there was a wind, it would have kept them from being such an issue. I filmed this flag waving for about six minutes. I even panned to other flags of the same kind and they were hanging on their sticks limp, no movement at all for any of them. Even the large flags that are on twenty-five foot poles were just lying there with no activity at all.

Yet again, in June of 2003, I had one of my most fantastic experiences that I have ever had while visiting Lakeview. I witnessed a full-bodied apparition. This "person" was just as plain to see as anyone you would ever meet. He was wearing 1920s-era clothing that I can still see today when I recall the experience. His hat was of the touring cap design. His shirt was all white and came complete with the puffy upper arms and the tighter cuffs. His pants were knickers and dark in color, a kind of ruddy brown hue in fact. This gentleman was actually locking up the gates at Lakeview, and believe it or not, it really upset me. He finished locking up the gates, and when he was done, he turned around and walked across the dirt road that led to the cemetery. When he reached the other side, he did something that most average people don't do—he disappeared!

I was astounded at what I had just witnessed because I then realized that this was a ghost and not a caretaker actually locking the gates—well, at least not from current day, anyway. I immediately drove up to the gates (I was sitting about twenty-five yards away in the van when I witnessed this) and found that the gates I had paid little attention to previously were rusted, broken, and falling off of their hinges. In my opinion, it would take someone a considerable amount of time and work to ever get them working properly again.

It is strange, when you first witness an apparition of this nature; it seems to take a considerable amount of time for it to "sink in." I think that this is a very good reason as to why a lot of encounters with the paranormal are simply buried in the back of the mind and passed off as hallucination or some other mundane occurrence. Had I not witnessed him disappearing for myself, I may have thought that it was just a person out there and not given it another thought. Of course, the clothing didn't register right away with me, but once it did, that was another clue as to what I had actually witnessed.

Being that Lakeview Cemetery has been studied by our group for many years, we have had requests from people to take them there. Either they don't believe that it is all that haunted, they don't believe in ghosts in general, or they are just curious to see the place that carries so many people into the realm of the paranormal.

On one occasion, a lady from Minneapolis wanted to see this cemetery for herself. I met and talked with her several times on www.ghostvillage.com. We set a date for her to drive the three and a half hours to see the cemetery that she had heard so much about. Well, the weather did not cooperate with us that night. It began to rain. Normally, we would cancel our trip when bad weather developed, but we didn't want this poor lady to drive a total of seven hours and not even get to see the cemetery. So, like a resourceful paranormal investigator, I decided that it would be a great time to take some comparison shots of rain. I hadn't done this very much prior to this time, but it seemed like a good opportunity to do some experimentation.

We loaded into the van and drove out to Lakeview. We weren't disappointed either! We still had strange occurrences, even though the weather was not conducive to paranormal investigation. Rhonda, my wife and Senior Investigator, was with us that night and she encountered something that she had never experienced before—smells. These smells were very strong and she was unable to identify them. This seemed very strange to us since it was raining. Usually, rain will knock smells out of the air, or at least keep them from traveling very far. Still, to this day, she has not encountered a smell like the ones she experienced that night.

Our guest and I also had an experience. While standing in the same general area as Rhonda and discussing the smells that she was receiving, we heard a small girl start coughing. This was only heard by our guest and me, and not by Rhonda. It was a very strange incident, indeed.

Yet another oddity that exists in this strange cemetery is a concrete angel. This is located in the very same area where the smells and little girl coughing were encountered. This angel gives every visitor the creeps when they arrive. It has eyes that follow you around the cemetery and almost seems like some kind of guardian of the dead.

We did have a strange occurrence with this simple statue. We had just arrived to the cemetery for a little evidence collection and were using the infrared thermometer as we do normally in all of our investigations. Keeping in mind that we live in northern Minnesota and it was during the fall of the year when this occurred, we captured a temperature anomaly that to this day still has us all puzzled. The ambient air temperature was about forty-eight degrees on this particular evening, and it had been a very sunny clear day with relatively low humidity. The high for the day was about sixty-eight degrees or so. When we started taking readings not long after sundown, the tombstones were all at about the same temperature—around sixty-three degrees—as was the bizarre angel statue.

Standing around talking a little bit about the "game plan" and how we wanted to investigate that night, we were astonished to find that the temperature of the angel had begun to rise. We watched it for several minutes with the infrared thermometer, and it reached a final temperature of seventy-three degrees. All other stones were still dropping in temperature, as one would expect with the sun down, bringing cooler air.

The angel stayed at about seventy-three degrees for a short period of time and then began to drop. It took it quite a while, but by the time we left that night, it had finally dropped down to the other stones in the cemetery and was the same temperature. (We don't use this as paranormal evidence, but it was a fantastic experience, and being that the word *paranormal* means "above normal," it would make it a paranormal experience.) Did a ghost cause it? I have no idea, but it was very interesting to say the least!

There is yet another strange area that we as paranormal investigators cannot explain, and that is the sanctuary. Okay, it isn't really called that by anyone but us—to the rest of the community it is known as the Veteran's Memorial. This memorial or *sanctuary* acts very strangely on most of our visits there. It is generally warmer. We obtain no paranormal evidence of any kind there—no EVPs, photographs, or videos, nothing whatsoever. Upon stepping out of the sanctuary, the temperature drops again and the paranormal activity is back to "normal." A road in the front, a row of very large pine trees on both sides, and a white picket fence in the rear of the area border this small region. It has a number of wooden, white crosses in the foreground of the area and a large crucifix-style statue toward the rear.

We don't know why the area behaves the way it does, but when we get tired of ghosts touching us, talking to us—whatever the case may be—we find a little solace by retreating into our little area known as the sanctuary. It is kind of like reaching the porch in a game of tag when you were a kid.

Lakeview Cemetery is not a place that you want to visit if you are faint of heart. And it can be a very terrifying place to spend a late night. There are noises, smells, shadows, and even an occasional apparition to put a little scare into you. Why is it so actively haunted? I believe Potter's Field is the reason, along with the lack of identity of the Shaw Hospital patients—but no one can say for sure. All I can tell you is this: If you find yourself in the middle of the Lakeview Cemetery some night with an angel statue staring you down and a smell you can't identify permeating your nostrils, you know that you will be taking something away with you that night—a fantastic paranormal experience that you will never forget.

Bright orb photograph taken in Lakeview Cemetery. Although many attempts were made to reproduce this orb, none were successful. *Photo taken by Brian Leffler*

An unexplained energy anomaly photographed in the Lakeview Cemetery. This photo was sent to the University of Minnesota and confirmed to not be an insect of any kind. *Photo taken by Brian Leffler*

Chapter Two
A Sad Story

Travis and April live in a quaint little house on the east side of Hibbing. It is very nicely decorated and very comfortable. They live there with their little dog that is very cute, but goes completely out of its mind when strangers show up—and of course, ghosts.

They had experienced a few things that seemed odd in the home, but never really gave it much thought until one night in April of 2005 when they both felt like there was something very uneasy in the air. Feeling disturbed by the feeling, they decided to get out of the house for a while. When they returned, everything seemed normal to them, and they went about their business, doing what a lot of skeptical people do—just putting it to the back of their minds. They really never gave much credence to ghosts and hauntings until they found out that their friend, Gina Hill, a member of the Northern Minnesota Paranormal Investigators, began discussing ghosts.

Front of April's home that was taken the night of our investigation. *Photo taken by Brian Leffler.*

The initial report to me was one of hearing a few footsteps and occasionally dealing with misplaced items such as the car keys. They also claimed that this usually only occured within the month of April. Gina had relayed this information to me, and needless to say, I didn't get overly excited about the house. It seemed to me that there wasn't a lot of activity, and it might very well be a waste of time to investigate it. Because Gina is a member of our group and a friend, however, we decided to go check out the house anyway. We are very happy that we did!

When we first arrived at the house and got our equipment inside, Christy and Kyle of our group both felt the presence of spirits in the home. Christy said that she felt the presence of an old woman and a young girl, while Kyle picked up on the spirit of an older gentleman. Both of them got feelings that were quite strong, and this marked the beginning of an adventure that wouldn't be soon forgotten by any of us.

The problems started with simple equipment failures that *can* happen, but usually don't in this many items all at once. One of our cameras, that had just been equipped with a brand new battery, failed first. The indicator light turned bright red, where it was usually a soft orange. Okay, so it changed color, not that unusual; but then the flash was very sporadic, it seemed to go off arbitrarily instead of when it was supposed to. (Sure, cameras can have failures like this, but since that time, the camera has worked fine with no problems at all.) We used one of my other cameras and didn't have any more problems.

The next equipment failure episode came with my VCR. Unknown to me was the fact that it wasn't recording throughout the entire time there. I had set up the camera, VCR, and television monitor, recorded a few seconds of Kyle upstairs in front of the camera and then viewed what had been recorded. It was set up correctly or I never would have captured this footage of Kyle waving. I set the VCR to record again and, you guessed it, it spent the entire time *not* recording, even though the typical "REC" came up on the screen, as well as displaying the little red LED light by the word "record." We have not figured out what happened or how this was even possible.

Yet another strange thing happened to an infrared thermometer. About half way through the investigation, this thermometer started beeping loudly at us from my toolbox where it was sitting inside the equipment box. Once I finally figured out what was making the noise, I pulled it from the box and found a temperature reading of 1026 degrees Fahrenheit. Hmmm, maybe the battery was bad. I changed out the battery for a new one and got the exact same reaction from the thermometer. Okay, now I know what you are thinking, "The thermometer has a problem." Well, I took the battery out of the thermometer thinking exactly that and put it back into the box and forgot about it for the rest of the night. The next day I went out, put the second battery back into the unit, and it worked perfectly.

But this chapter is titled, A Sad Story in Hibbing, Minnesota. Though the equipment failures we experienced that night were sad to us, they were not the sadist part of the story. The title is held by the story of Gene and his two daughters. This story is incomplete and a little sketchy at best, but what we *do* know is heartbreaking. Gene was a hard-working father who really had nothing but his two daughters. "That is a lot to have," you may say, but he couldn't provide entirely well for them. You see, Gene lived in the basement of this house at one time. He rented the area, and it was only large enough for his bed and some clothing, and not much more. His daughters lived upstairs where they shared a room. One night, Gene died leaving his two daughters all alone with no apparent relatives. We have not been able to find any more information out about Gene or his two daughters because he was a renter in this house. There are no records available for any member of that family. We do firmly believe that Gene and at least one of his daughters are still residing in Hibbing.

Is it Gene that haunts the electrical equipment of this home? Are the disappearing items a prank by Gene's daughter? We may never know...

Anomaly that was captured at the bottom of the stairs in April's house.
Photo taken by Kyle Bruzenak.

Chapter Three
Moon Lake

Moon lake is place of many mysteries as well as many spirits. This old piece of property holds many riddles, and I believe that we have only scratched the surface as to what is really going on with this house and property.

The original house on the property is almost a hundred years of age. It was purchased from the State of Minnesota in about 1911 or 1912—the historical record is a little cloudy as to the exact date of the transfer. I did look at an old photograph of the land and original house, and it was just your basic barren grassland with a small house and a couple of small cabins. It really didn't look like much at that time, but believe me, it has flourished into a fantastic homestead over the many years.

The front of the Harvey home that sits on the property on the shores of Moon Lake.
Photo taken by Brian Leffler.

In the early days of the property, it was a logging camp. From what Christy picked up there psychically during our visit, a man who was not overly pleasant to work for, ran it. I am sure that the conditions at an old, turn-of-the-century logging camp were not the best for people to endure. I am also sure that disease and the elements were responsible for many deaths on the property at that time. Does this type of setting leave an imprint on the land itself? I certainly believe that it does. I would be willing to bet my bottom dollar that this will be the source of future problems of this place.

The property remained in the Johnson family for many years, until the death of Carl Johnson. It was at that time that the Depaul family inherited the land from Carl and maintained the home property until the time that they decided to sell it in the early 1990s.

Chris and Beth Harvey live on the homestead now with their two children, Abby and Spencer. They bought the property in 1992. That year, Chris began working feverishly to complete the beautiful home that now stands on the property on the shores of Moon Lake. Chris built his home with the utmost attention to detail, using brick on the exterior and many different beautiful materials on the inside of the home. There is natural oak wherever you look in the house, it is very well decorated, and a very comfortable place to spend time with family.

One Potato, Two….

There is one small problem though; Chris built the house right on top of Carl Johnson's potato garden—the *same* potato garden where Carl Johnson's family spread his ashes after having him cremated. It would seem that Carl loved his garden so much that he wanted to remain with it into eternity.

We all want to leave our mark on the world and we all crave to have some sort of recognition that we were here on Earth. I believe that this is really no different than building over top an Indian burial site or a cemetery that had the markers moved but the bodies remaining in the same location. Even though Carl's physical body was incinerated, it is still what he has for remains.

This protection or watching over a spirit's physical remains are what I think brings spirits back into cemeteries. I have heard many times from various paranormal investigators as well as psychics that it makes no sense to them as to why a spirit would linger in a cemetery. It makes perfect sense to me that they would want to keep some sort of tie between the spiritual state that they are currently in and the physical state that they used to be in. It is probably due to a certain amount of selfishness on the part of our own psyche that gives our spirit a longing for this connection, and thus explains why there is a large amount of activity quite often reported and collected from within a cemetery. Since this case concerning Carl Johnson is no different, and this site is his "grave" (so to speak), it makes sense that as soon as the house was built over his gravesite, the spirit of Carl would haunt it from that day forward.

Beth told me that one of the earliest oddities with the house concerned baby spoons. You see, her children Abby and Spencer are twins. They usually had double of everything, and in most cases, they had four or five of each thing to make sure they didn't run out of it at a crucial time. After all, there is no corner convenience store down the block that is open in the middle of the night when you live on at the end of an old dirt road in the woods. She had the spoons on a rack so that she could get to them easily enough holding two babies in her arms. These spoons would be constantly disappearing from this rack.

Beth did call her mother, at one point, to see if she could offer any suggestion about where these spoons could have been disappearing. Her mother offered the only logical explanation that she could think of—perhaps they were falling down inside the cushions of the furniture. All of the furniture was checked thoroughly, and not one spoon was ever found there. The only people in the house at the time were Chris, Beth, and the two babies—so they weren't being taken by anyone who was living. Beth feels that these spoon incidents are related to Carl Johnson and could very well be his way of making his presence known in the house.

Other things also came up missing at different times. Chris, while still building the house, lost a hand saw and square that he had just been using—it seemed to suddenly disappear. Neither the tools nor the baby spoons have ever been found.

One day, not long after the family moved into the house, Spencer brought some old Indian artifacts to Beth. One appeared to be a rock that was once used as a tool. Beth wanted to find out just where Spencer was getting these objects, and he told her that he had found them over by the garage. One day, while exploring the old garage, she heard a voice. This voice did not seem exceptionally friendly, nor did it really want her in that location. It yelled for her to "get out!" She did as the voice commanded.

Immediately, she approached Chris and asked him if he was yelling at her, to which he said, "No." She then asked, "Were you yelling at the chickens?" He responded with yet another "no." It was at that moment that Beth realized that a ghostly voice had yelled for her to get out of the garage. It was quite some time before she could muster up the courage to face this building again. She began to have nightmarish visions about the building, seeing it oozing blood from the seams of the building itself. She knew from these visions that something bad had happened within the confines of that old garage.

This is also where Beth discovered that she was more in-tune with her general surroundings. She realized that she was given psychic gifts. A friend of hers was involved with doing what is called

"Soul Rescue" and they put Beth and Chris on the right track to having this done to see if they could get a little more information about what had occurred in the garage. This event that gave Beth a very uneasy feeling of dread. Beth did feel that someone had died in this garage.

Beth and Chris went to Duluth where they met with the people from "Soul Rescue." There was a woman there who was a psychic medium—a channeler actually—and she channeled the spirit of a man named John Jacob Johnson who had taken his own life. It is believed that he committed this act in the early 1930s during the depression, but with the shaky historical record, it is very difficult to pinpoint an exact date at this time.

The medium discovered during this session that Johnson was tired of being cold all the time, having no money, and the drinking and fighting that went on almost constantly. Once he'd had enough, he'd gone to the garage and hanged himself from one of the two large hooks that hung from the ceiling in the old building. (The medium also reported that the land itself was very rich with spirits.) Those hooks are still located there today.

Unfortunately, the historical record is a bit shady where the young man was concerned. I am currently attempting to find out about his death and what happened that made him cut his life short so tragically. One other thing that I find very interesting about John Jacob Johnson is that he is not known to be on any family tree to date. It almost seems like he was either someone who family wanted to forget or perhaps someone who was not related to the family of the property owners—which is a strong possibility since Johnson is a very common surname in the northern woods of Minnesota. Since there are no death records with this name on them, is it possible that the family, all these years ago, could have laid him to rest on the property? There weren't nearly as tight a control on situations like this back in those days, and it would be possible that a family paid their last respects and were distraught enough to want to bury him on the family land so that they could be close for generations to come.

Chris went on to explain that almost from day one of living in their new house, he would see the semi-formed apparition of a tall man walking in the house. This would take place primarily in the main living room—and he has seen it very frequently. He believes this is also the spirit of Carl Johnson, doing his rounds through the house that now sits on top of his grave.

Open Sesame and a Sense of Humor

Though there is a ton of master craftsmanship and love put into this house, there is a drawer in the kitchen that is a riddle to the family. It opens by itself on almost a regular basis when the family comes into the kitchen. They are forever closing this pesky drawer. Chris has adjusted it to its maximum adjustment to where while opening the drawer, you are almost pulling it up at somewhat of an angle to open it, and yet it defies everything natural in the world and remains open when it wants to be open. It cannot be attributed to any slope in the cabinet, since the other drawers on either side of this anomaly remain closed at all times, unless the family opens them. To this day, the entire family has shut this drawer so many times that it has almost become a natural act for them to do so. This kind of phenomena will happen somewhat frequently, and then, when the family gets a little tired of it happening, they will tell the spirits in their house to "knock it off," and it will stop for a period of time. It always, to the frustration of the family, starts up again just as suddenly as it stops.

On the garage end of the house there is a laundry room and bathroom that has been added onto the house since the original building in 1992. This room seems to come complete with its own set of ghostly problems that don't occur anywhere else in the house.

The faucet for the bathroom sink will turn on and stay on until someone goes in and shuts it off. I have to tell you that when I was at this house conducting the interview for this book, I used that sink and these knobs were pretty tight to turn. Of course, your first impression of this type of phenomena would be that the knobs are wearing out and perhaps a little bit loose, and that it is all due to the water pressure. Well, it can't be—this faucet is very tight and new. I cannot see this knob turning on its own in any way other than a gasket failing, and then you would not be able to turn the water off at all, other than the shut-off valve under the sink.

Aside from the water coming on, there would seem to be a practical joker spirit in the house that likes to be a nuisance—without doing any real damage to the house. This particular spirit loves to go in this same bath and laundry room and unroll the toilet paper all over the floor. Of course, the family gets a little bit frustrated at trying to roll the paper back up on the roll, which we all know is a very wearisome task to say the least.

On yet another occasion, Abby had an encounter with someone who was dressed all in black clothing. He was wearing a black hat, shirt, pants, and shoes—all jet black. She said that he always keeps his head down, looking at the ground when he walks. This spirit is one that is new in the house according to Abby, and he is also the spirit that plays with the faucet in the bath and laundry room. She simply refers to this spirit as "The Producer." When she first saw him he was coming up the walkway into the house and he went straight for the bath and laundry room area of the house. It is almost humorous that a spirit would show this kind of behavior, and head directly for that room. Nobody knows why, but he doesn't seem to be scary at all, just a little bit of a nuisance, since he likes to turn on the water and let it run until someone comes along to turn it off.

Basement Fear!

The guest bedroom in the basement seems to be a very active spot in the house and is even a very scary spot for some. Abby has described a little girl spirit by the name of Sarah who lives in the guest bedroom tucked away in the basement. Sarah is seen frequently wearing a long white gown and has long blonde hair. Abby participates in a dance line through the computer located in the basement, and she will be asked frequently by Sarah if she will show her how to dance like that. Sarah also wants to know how the entire computer program itself works.

One day, not too long ago, the family decided that they would sage the house since they had heard that it would cleanse the home of bad spirits, allowing only the good ones to remain. While using the sage in the basement, Abby was confronted by Sarah. Sarah asked, "What are you doing?" Abby replied, "We are using sage in the house to make sure that the bad spirits leave the house." Sarah then replied, "But I am not a bad spirit," "can I still live here?" Abby told her that of course she could stay in the house, to which Sarah asked, "Is it okay if I keep living in the bedroom?" Abby told her that would be fine and that she could stay as long as she liked in their house.

The guest bedroom has also not been a very friendly spot for Beth's sister who had come to visit them on a couple of occasions. It would have been more often over the years, but due to her experiences in the bedroom, she refuses to stay in the house any more. Her first experience occurred when she sat down on the edge of the bed in the room and immediately felt a pair of hands around her throat choking her! She was absolutely terrified as, of course, she could not identify her attacker, nor could she even see any part of this assailant. She ran upstairs, and since Chris was again working on a midnight shift, she climbed into bed with Beth where she spent the remainder of the night.

Her second experience occurred very late one night after she had gotten the courage again to try to stay in the basement bedroom. She stayed awake until total exhaustion consumed her body. She was very afraid to go back into the basement to try sleeping in the bedroom where she'd been choked initially during her first visit. She had finally been exhausted to the point where she was partially willing to go into the basement to sleep, but only after she made Beth go down first to turn on the radio and all of the lights. She went down the stairs saying, "I hate sleeping here."

Beth decided that she just knew something was going to happen, so she stayed up a little longer to see if anything would cause her sister to come running out of that haunted basement. It took only a short while for that incident to take place as Beth had predicted. A horribly loud noise, sounding like something very large and heavy, fell on the floor almost next to Beth and right above her sister in the bed downstairs. Beth jumped almost out of her skin, as she was half asleep in the chair, but her sister screamed and came running out of the basement just as fast as she possibly could run. She said, "That's it, no more!" And she has not returned to spend the night with their family in this house since. Perhaps if the Harvey family ever does sell the house and move, they will be able to receive more visits from Beth's sister.

It would seem that either the spirits don't like Beth's sister, or they just don't like anyone sleeping in the guest bedroom. They haven't really had anyone else visiting who has attempted to sleep in the room other than Abby's friend, Sammi, so they wonder if there would be similar problems with the room under other circumstances.

Abby and her girlfriend, Sammi, slept in the basement one night and had an encounter with Carl. While the girls were attempting to sleep, Carl came out and appeared to them in a black and red-checkered shirt—complete with suspenders. The girls also reported that he had a big belly. He stood in the doorway of the gray room for a while just watching the girls before he finally retreated back into the room that is considered by the family to be *his room*. The Gray Room is called that because it is the only unfinished room in the basement and has the standard concrete floor that is painted with gray paint. Thus, the family had dubbed Carl's room "the Gray Room."

Beth also reports seeing what she calls "blips" of energy in the house. She has said that she sees them almost on a constant basis and is unsure just what they are. I would have to consider these "blips" to be orbs. Our group has proven, in the year 2006, that orbs are related to the paranormal, so even though I have not seen these "blips," as Beth describes them, I would have to put my money on orbs being what she is seeing around the house.

Beth also reports that the family hears a "ping" noise at the locations of electrical plugs throughout the house. This is described as a very weird phenomena, and I must admit, one that I have personally never heard of in all of my years as a paranormal investigator. As far as electrical issues go, one morning they all awoke to loud music playing and every light in the house on. All four of the family members woke up at the same time to witness this phenomena. Additionally, every alarm clock was blinking as if there had been a power outage during the night.

An Energetic Ghost

One night, Beth was awakened by a strong magnetic energy. She was in bed alone, as Chris was working a midnight shift and not in the house. Waking up in a panic, as she did not know what was going on, she immediately called her girlfriend who lives in Duluth and explained to her that this energy woke her from a dead sleep. Her girlfriend told her that, though she was unsure about the energy that woke her friend up, there was another strange thing. She advised that she didn't have her *own* phone line, but the phone line of a James Klause. They thought this was a very odd thing, indeed, but by the end of the conversation, ended up tucking it in the back of their minds. While not forgetting about it, they simply chalked it up to a weird thing and didn't worry about it.

The next morning, the girlfriend called Beth to inform her that James Klause was no longer among the living at the time and during the prior night when Mrs. Klause picked up her phone, ending up talking with both Beth and her girlfriend. The woman was calling her daughter and didn't expect to find two people talking on the line at the same time *she* was on the line.

They discussed how strange this was and determined that Beth had Mrs. Klauses' phone line and Mrs. Klause had Beth's line. The phone company would need to be called to see what was going on—and that is when things got even stranger for them. The phone company had to *physically switch* the wires back in the box. *The wires had been switched.* The night before everything had been okay, and it wasn't until Beth was awakened by this energy that they made the discovery in the first place.

There is still one more odd twist of fate relating to this part of the story. Beth's girlfriend, a few days later, ended up with the phone line belonging to the local beauty shop down the street with the same situation of the wires being physically crossed requiring physical switching by the phone company.

Was this a prank? Did someone with a lot of knowledge about phone lines and their junction boxes decide in the middle of the night to play a joke on these poor unsuspecting people—and then drive to Duluth to pull the same prank on Beth's girlfriend? I do have my doubts that someone went to those great lengths to pull this type of prank—which isn't really all that funny. Could it have been a spirit playing a joke on them? Certainly it could have been. This, of course, is just another in a long line of ghostly encounters that have been attributed to the spirit-rich atmosphere in the Harvey home at Moon Lake.

There is one incident that really stands out for the Harveys concerning appliances and electricity. This one particular morning had to be the worst that anyone could imagine. When they woke up, they discovered that their kitchen stove had melted. It was totally fried. They could not figure out what happened, as the stove was not very old and they didn't smell burning. But all of the wiring inside the stove was melted and useless; they were forced to buy a new stove as the repairs would have cost almost as much as having it fixed. (Isn't that the way things usually are in our disposable world?)

The stove incident was bad enough, but to add insult to injury, there were yet two other things that went haywire electrically that morning. The family's water pump decided that it would also go belly up and need replacing. It seemed to be a good morning for it to short out and quit working. There also was a light bulb that literally exploded.

The power company was called out and performed an electrical check of all the lines, the transformer, and everything else that was running to the house—including the meter. Everything checked out fine with flying colors. There were no problems outside the home that would have caused all of this damage. Then, an electrician was called to check everything on the inside of the house. He checked the breaker box and the home's wiring, but found there to be no problems at all.

This morning's disasters had no rational explanation for anything that had occurred. In the end, the family bought a new stove, a new water pump, and replaced the wire from the pump to the house, as it was also shorted and melted.

In a different year, 1996, there was another electrical malfunction where the vent hood that hung over their island stove blew out while Beth was cooking a meal. This was a frightening experience as Beth was standing directly under it using the stove when it happened. Again, there were no rational explanations for any of these things to be occurring in their home. Heck, this house wasn't that old and had all new building materials, in addition to meeting all of the modern code requirements.

Can ghosts do this kind of damage? I believe that they can. I have seen spirits mess with all different kinds of electrical devices, and our team even had an experience with an electronic device malfunction—but I will get to that when I start talking about the actual investigation our team conducted in this house.

Beth tells of an interesting and yet sad story of who she believes is one of the spirits in the house. She is constantly feeling a spirit that comes to sit on her lap whom she believes is the spirit of a little boy. Both Abby and another psychic have described this little boy. He is described as being around four or five years of age with dark skin, Mulatto, in fact. He wears bib overalls with a white t-shirt underneath, and red-tied shoes. It wasn't until a psychic described the little boy and pointed to a photograph of the boy's sister that it really clicked with Beth as to who this was running around her house. It was her nephew, Peter.

Now, Peter met with a tragic end to his very short life. He was a murder victim in Duluth some years ago. He was about twenty years old when this happened. A dreadful end to a very nice boy who had all the dreams of leaving his mark on this world, but never really got the chance to do that. I know what you are thinking: If he was killed at about age twenty, how could he be the little boy running around the house out at Moon Lake? I believe that there doesn't have to be a tragic end for a spirit to linger among the living, I firmly believe that they can go to a place and/or time that they were happiest in their lives. I don't believe that they have to stay exactly where they were in the physical world until they are ready to be re-born and start over. I think that they can go to that happy place, and while there, can change how they appear to whatever they wish to be. Perhaps it depends on their mood at the time. It is Beth's very strong belief that this little boy running around her house is her nephew, Peter, and with all of the independent descriptions and the photograph of him that I saw, I think that it is a very good possibility that Peter is lingering in a place that made him exceptionally happy with people that made him just as content.

Witch Way Did They Go?

On one of the occasions where there were electrical problems, Beth had another fairly strange experience. The electrician who came to the house asked her if she were able to "witch" for water? This was a very odd comment to come from a guy who was there to take a look at the electrical system, but he and Beth began talking about the subject, and as it turned out, the electrician's grandmother was able to "witch" or divine for water.

This was thought provoking for Beth and she decided that she would learn more about the subject. After reading several books on the subject, she decided that she would give it a try by making a couple of divining rods out of old metal coat hangers—and she found that it worked for her. This is also the time frame in which she learned about water and electricity and how it relates to the paranormal world.

It would seem that Abby and Sammi ventured into the old house that still stands on the property, the original homestead. They reported seeing an old man whom they described as being scruffy and dirty with a beard. With him in the house were two small girls clothed in dresses. The old man told the girls (the living ones) that they needed to get out of that house, that nobody needs to be in that house. The girls then told the old man that they could come in the house any time they wanted, and the reaction from the old man was not too pleasant! Evidently, in order to get his point across to them, he began to use some very foul language and yelled at them enough that they immediately left.

When they told Beth what had happened, she made the decision that they were to stay out of that house from then on—since they didn't have need to be exposed to that sort of behavior, even if it was from some old, dirty, scruffy dead man.

There are several trails that run through the woods behind the home where occasionally, on a nice day, Abby will walk and explore, just like any kid her age would do. The difference is when she walks this trail, she picks up the presence of an old Indian chief who is residing on this part of the property. He has told her not only that the Ojibwa Indians settled on this land, but relayed some of their history, like how the women used to sit in circles to do their daily work, such as cooking, sewing, and related tasks. He told her how the Indians would use the lake for their water supply and instructed her about an old burial site back behind the trees.

This burial site is not a mound and it is no longer marked in any way, but it does exist in the woods somewhere. The family has no idea where this spot is located, but it would seem that the family dog has begun to be afraid of something on this part of the land. The dog used to walk all over with Chris, but now she will only go as far as the power line that runs through the property and she refuses to go any further. If Chris goes further, she will wait for him to return and begin walking with him again as soon as he crosses back over the power line. This behavior is not something that has been normal for her, but rather something that has begun only recently. No matter how much Chris calls her, she will, in the end, win the battle and refuse to follow him into that part of the woods.

Is this the location of the burial site? I, of course, am not sure, but since animals tend to be much more in-tune with their surroundings and follow much keener senses than humans do, perhaps there really are the spirits of long dead Ojibwa Indians located in those woods, and this may be the reason that the family dog wants no part of that area. It does seem that their dog is tuned into the spirits, as there are many times the family will see her staring or barking at things that aren't there. There are also times that she will be sitting in the living room during the middle of the night crying. Chris gets up and checks on her and she is always fine. This behavior is something that I find to be quite typical in haunted locations that have animals.

Again, outside in the summer of 2006, Chris was sitting by himself on the deck just relaxing and taking in some starlight. The rest of the family had already gone to bed for the night. While sitting there, Chris heard a voice call out quite loudly three times in a row: "Uncle John." He never saw anyone and never heard anything else that night that would suggest that someone *living* would have been there on the property with him. Chris decided quite quickly that he had had enough for the evening and retired to the sanctity of his own bedroom.

The Moon Lake property has many different outbuildings located on it and some of those buildings are cabins located directly against the shores of Moon Lake itself. One of those cabins, the one near the sauna, is one that Abby has reported seeing an older schoolteacher residing within. She sees her wearing a long dress and wire-rimmed glasses. During the investigations that the family has done into the history of the place, they discovered that when the Depaul family owned the land, their Aunt would come and visit, spending the entire summer when off from school. It was also discovered that the cabin near the sauna was the cabin in which she stayed on her many repeated trips to the area. She had a large brass bed placed there that was high enough so that she could lie on the bed and watch the lake. Recently, there have been several separate instances of Beth and Abby going into the cabin to find small piles of pencil shavings on the floor. These were never there before, but it sure seems like something that you may expect to find in the cabin of an English teacher.

Lofty Ghosts

The barn is yet another outbuilding that has had its fair share of paranormal experiences. Abby and her friend, Sammi, like to go into the old building and up into the loft area to play. They love the loft but are afraid of it, so they make Beth go up there with them and sit there while they play. On one of their ventures into this loft, they made the discovery that there were two little girls there with them—well their spirits, anyway. They were ages six and eight. They have told the girls that there was a train that crashed in the area many, many years ago that killed their entire family. Their parents' spirits are not on the property but the two little girls stay in the barn because they like it there. Sadly, they have nothing to remember their mother by with one exception. The only possession that they have of hers is the blue hem of her dress. When you go into the loft area in the back corner, there is a piece of blue material that could very well have belonged to the hem of a dress. This could also be the reason that the girls' spirits are remaining in the area. They could be attached to this one physical object that perhaps did belong to their mother whom they miss tremendously.

One day after arriving home from school, Abby told her mother, "There is a woman in the loft with a mole on her face that keeps looking out the window." Before she could get all of the words out, Beth had a flash through her mind of Jackie Kennedy. She isn't really sure as to why this image would flash into her mind, but it did. A day or two later, Beth was pulling up a photo of Jackie Kennedy on her computer and Abby saw it. She said, "That's her! That's the lady that was in the barn!" Beth told her that this was Jackie Kennedy.

While in the barn, Abby and Sammi called upon Jackie Kennedy and asked why she would be in the barn. Apparently Jackie is said to have replied, "I just like it there."

This leads to an answer of another strange occurrence within the house walls. It would seem that the family had been finding many black and yellow feathers around the house, and Jackie states that she is the one who has been dropping those feathers.

Additionally, there have been several reports of a man fitting the description of Abraham Lincoln in the house, as well as Marilyn Monroe and Judy Garland (who is said to be Abby's spirit guide). There is no apparent reason for these famous people to be haunting the Moon Lake property, so it makes me wonder what exactly is happening and why these ghosts are appearing in this manner.

It is possible that, for some reason, Beth and Abby—being of strong psychic ability—draw the spirits of these people to them like a beacon of understanding and a place that they can contact the living and be heard. Or are they simply other ghosts using the visage of these dead famous people, perhaps as somewhat of a prank? I also have to wonder if Abby isn't able to channel the spirits of these people and bring them in to communicate with her. I suppose that whatever the scenario, it is quite possible that any are true. But no matter what the real reason, the family is seeing these spirits in this form on some occasions.

The Here and Now for the Hereafter

The family had a recent encounter and, in fact, their *first* encounter of actually witnessing a moving object. It would seem that, recently, there was a ghost in their den area that decided it would be a great time to send the television remote flying into the middle of the room. The remote was sitting on the couch; it lifted up, did a flip, and ended up in the middle of the floor.

Beth's deceased dad is also said to be in the house. The family always knows when he is making himself known to them. When he is there, the family will smell the strong odor of whiskey. Beth's dad died in 1999, and she was there with him at his deathbed. She knew immediately when his spirit left the physical world and crossed into the spirit world. He has been with her ever since that day.

The Investigation

The Northern Minnesota Paranormal Investigators (N.M.P.I.) became involved with the Harvey family around Halloween of 2005. We had done several interviews for newspapers and radio, and the Harveys had heard of us through the media. They sent us an email and began telling us about the things that have gone on in their home. Of course, they didn't tell us all of it at that time, but they told us enough to peak our interest in doing an investigation. We went to investigate the house on November 20, 2005. It was kind of a strange coincidence, but when I went back to interview Beth and Chris for this book, it happened to be exactly one year later to the day.

Arriving in the early evening, we set up our equipment and began investigating. One of the reports we had was of Abby's room, probably the hottest spot in the house. I set up the one security camera that we had at the time in her room. Our security camera set up was quite primitive then in comparison to what it is now, but thanks to this room and this camera set up, we learned just how we needed to fine tune the system for the best results in future investigations. You see, what happened to us in this room had never happened before, and to this date, has never happened since.

We used to have our system set up with both the camera and the VCR in the same room as we were using the red, yellow, and white plugs from the camera directly into the VCR. To run hundreds of feet of this type of cord would be very expensive and not overly practical. I had gone into the bedroom and Kyle was watching the television, guiding me into the best place to capture the largest portion of the room. I had set up the VCR and turned it to record. Kyle was able to see "REC" on the screen of the monitor, so we were able to verify that it was recording. When we watched the tape afterward, it turned out that it had recorded absolutely nothing in Abby's room, but when we moved the camera to the master bedroom it recorded flawlessly.

There was nothing in the set up done differently at either time for the recording sessions, but for some reason, even though we could both verify that the VCR was recording, we produced no videotape of Abby's room. With the extensive reports of electrical problems and meltdowns in the home, we don't doubt that the spirits in her room were not wanting to be seen on camera, so they messed with the equipment, not allowing any recording in that room. We have since refined the set up of these security cameras and VCRs so that we convert the signal to a coaxial cable with an RF box and run the coax back to the VCR, which is sitting at the table with the monitor. The only piece of equipment that is placed into the area being recorded is the camera itself on the tripod. We have not had this same problem since that change.

Once the camera had been moved to the master bedroom of the house, we were quite fortunate in what we captured on videotape. We actually captured a spirit in the room, as well as this particular spirit messing with our camera set up. After a considerable time of running the video, and with nobody allowed inside the room while taping, we captured a strange flash of light on the wall toward the right side of the frame.

Keep in mind that this home is located at the end of a dead-end driveway and there is no traffic using the driveway since there are several signs at the beginning of it warning would-be visitors that this is a private area. So the only visitors to the home are people who are intending on visiting the family. This eliminated car headlights as a possibility for the flash, but what was most interesting is the fact that immediately after the flash on the wall, the camera blanked out—for only a very fast three frames. The first and second frames were kind of a pinkish, salmon color that I'd never witnessed before, and the third one was black. The camera immediately regained function after these frames and captured an orb moving away from the camera and then disappearing. This video may be viewed at our website. Unfortunately, we were unable to capture it on film.

Our team had a very strange experience in the basement bedroom. We had our camcorder situated on the tripod for quite some time recording the bedroom that had displayed a lot of activity over the years. The bed was very neatly made, as Beth had just changed the sheets on it that morning and made the bed. We all saw that it was neatly made and had remained untouched since she'd made it.

About an hour after pulling the camera out of that room, we went back into the room to do some EVP recording and it was immediately noticed that the comforter on the bed and some pillows had been messed up. It appeared as if someone had been lying on the bed taking a nap. We had made sure that the family was "corralled" during the investigation and had asked them to not go anywhere without an investigator. In this way, we were able to verify where everyone was at any given time during the investigation. We have actual still photographs taken by team members that show the bed before and after—how it actually looked. It is very clear that when we started investigating it, the bed was very neatly made, and then after the camera was removed and people starting moving into the room for EVP work and photographing, the bed was messed up. There was nobody on our team who had been lying on the bed and no family members were in the basement at any time after we had begun our investigation.

One of my very favorite places on the property was inside the original, old house. We had an experience in there that I don't think that any of us will soon forget. When we walked into this dilapidated old house, we felt a sense of dread and oppression. It was a very heavy feeling that we all felt at the same time. We know that because we all reported this at once. We poked around a bit. It wasn't a large house, which is typical of the turn-of-the-century farmhouses in northern Minnesota. I was photographing in the building when, during one of my photos, the flash went off as it should, but I saw a bright red veil of a misty haze directly in front of my face. I mean right in front of me! It actually startled me for a split second and made me move backward half a step when I saw it.

The funny thing about this experience is that the other two investigators who were with me at the time saw two different things occurring at the same moment. One of them saw the top half of an old man and the other saw the entire body of an old man. Neither investigator saw the red haze that I saw. This makes me wonder about seeing apparitions. Does the angle and distance make a world of difference in how we see them? Possibly, but it is most likely, in my opinion, that the interpretation comes from within each of our brains, when the eyes record something.

It is something along the lines of a car accident when there are witnesses to the scene. These witnesses can give their statement to the police and every witness will have a slightly different version of what actually happened in the accident. This phenomenon has been very well documented over many years by most police agencies around the globe. Interpretation is the key, in my opinion. So, to remind everyone reading this, be respectful of others who view paranormal work. It all may come down to their interpretation, and it may vary greatly from what you see or hear in the evidence that you collect.

Probably one of the most fantastic experiences for the team was that several had seen, who they believe to be, Carl Johnson in the basement. They saw him in the Gray Room (of course), since that is considered to be his main territory. They watched him for quite a lengthy amount of time, making attempts to record his presence on film and audiotape—but it was to no avail. They were unable to capture the evidence needed from an investigation standpoint, but they were very much able to all be equally touched deep inside from his presence there. Nobody felt any maliciousness in the encounter, nor did they feel any fear. They actually felt kind of a sadness for the man. This was also the first time that Gina had seen a full-bodied apparition in her lifetime and that can be quite a moving experience on its own. (I will never forget that first time I witnessed an apparition of this nature for the very first time. It is a feeling that just suddenly washes over every inch of your being.)

At one point during the investigation, there were Chris, Kyle, another Chris (who wanted to join our group at the time), and myself standing in the barn's loft area. We were having a conversation, and, of course, had our tape recorders running, attempting to capture some EVP. We did make a capture. We caught what sounded like a girl's voice on the tape simply saying, "Hi." It was a lengthy EVP by any means, but it was a definite *Class A*. It rang through on the tape so clearly that it sent chills up my spine the very first time I listened to it. Was it one of the little girls who had lost her parents in the tragic train accident giving us a friendly greeting? Of course, it certainly could have been. It could also have been any one of the multitudes of spirits that linger on this property.

This investigation was a top favorite for the members of N.M.P.I. It was loaded with personal experience, as well as the collection of some pretty solid evidence that the land and home was haunted.

One of the main reasons that this family called us in the first place was that Abby was having a very difficult time sleeping in her room. Spirits almost constantly throughout the night were visiting her and they were keeping her awake. This lack of sleep was beginning to deteriorate her function at school and have an effect on her work. It was nice that we were able to help Abby out a bit, and give her some guidelines as to how to "shut off" her psychic ability so that she could get some sleep. Now, a year later, she is doing very well—she's kicked the spirits out of her room at night and reclaimed her territory!

All of the members of our group had a wonderful time during this investigation, and it was a very good feeling to come in and validate the paranormal phenomena for this very nice family.

Ectoplasm photographed inside the original house at Moon Lake.
Photo taken by Rhonda Leffler

Ectoplasm photographed inside the pole building located at Moon Lake.
Photo taken by Rhonda Leffler

Chapter Four
Old North Cemetery

As many of you may not know, Hibbing, Minnesota is forever known as "The Town That Moved." This was a result of the mining industry. When the digging was planned to begin on the Hull Rust Mine, they either had to move it or loose it. The Hull Rust Mine is one of the largest open-pit mines in the world, abundantly loaded with iron ore. The town of Hibbing was forced to re-locate itself, in large part because of the then blossoming city that would be taken over by the mine. Moving the town was not an overnight process; it began in about 1916, and ran through the 1950s. The heaviest push for the town movement occurred during both World War I and World War II, but a majority of businesses that moved did so during the year 1920.

Partial over-all view of the Old North Hibbing Cemetery photographed at dusk. *Photo taken by Brian Leffler*

The story of the Old North Hibbing Cemetery is a sad one. It was originally located at the end of what was Superior Street, which was just beyond the Catholic and Episcopal Churches. When the digging for the Hull Rust Mine began, the graves that were marked were moved quite easily—but that is not where I believe the story of ghosts in this cemetery begins. I believe that it is a direct result of non-marked graves and lost souls due to what I would have to call mishandling of the bodies once located in this hallowed ground.

As digging was begun in a new area, there was what was called "overburden" that had to be stripped away to get to the rich deposits of iron ore. This overburden was riddled with bones of people who were buried without an identity. Most of these discovered remains were buried in the cemetery in unmarked graves, again leaving these souls without identity. Many other remains were simply loaded into the ore carts and discarded with the overburden in the dump that now defines the Eastern edge of the city of Hibbing. I feel that the combination of these two factors is directly related to the amount of activity that is found on a regular basis in this cemetery.

The cemetery is not used anymore, and, in fact, the burials stopped there many years ago. It is not a large cemetery either, only perhaps one and a half football fields in either direction. At one point in its history, part of the cemetery caved in, exposing the caskets and bodies underneath the ground. This section lost many of its marker stones when this occurred and had to be filled in and the sod replaced.

The Old North Hibbing Cemetery is one of the first cemeteries I discovered and investigated during the early years of my paranormal research career. I really have enjoyed this cemetery, from the standpoint of an investigator, because it has provided me with a lot of evidence of ghosts. It has also been very interesting with its rich history. There is a strange mausoleum located here that is very simple in construction, but has a heavy steel door for access. This door had been welded shut long ago due to continuous vandalisms that have taken place. Legend has it that a grieving husband and father who buried his beloved wife there, sitting in her favorite rocking chair with their baby in her arms, constructed this mausoleum. It is rumored that the baby and the mother died during childbirth. This legend is what had spawned the vandalism of the small silver painted building. I have heard an eyewitness account from a reliable source that when she was a small girl, the door had come open. She saw inside and was able to confirm the legend.

As I said earlier, this is where I got my start in the paranormal field; aside from investigating the house in Chisholm where I once lived. This cemetery has provided many EVP, one of which I found to be very interesting. When I played back the tape originally, there was something that sounded like the scream of a woman. There were no women any where near me—I was alone in the cemetery at the time. It was right about dusk that I captured this. When I downloaded the audio into the computer and used my program to stretch it out, it began to take on an entirely different appearance. Then it began to sound like a man's voice that said, "Quarter to three." This recording is still among my favorites and can be heard on our website located at www.hauntingresearch.com.

Another very interesting phenomenon seen at this cemetery was the "angel picture" that my wife, Rhonda, captured there on her first paranormal investigation. It was her fourth photo taken on her first roll of film. When she looked at it she saw the form of an angel. Is this a case of matrixing? Do angels really exist? I can't say for sure, but she claims to have seen her guardian angel when she was a child and is a very strong believer in the existence of them.

This is one location that hasn't been visited by either my group or myself in a very long time, but I am thinking that another visit very soon just may be in order. Who knows, perhaps we will be able to eventually identify one of those lost souls that linger there. Perhaps they won't be able to cross over and move on until the time when their bodies receive the recognition deserved and are laid to rest properly. Will that ever be possible to happen? I doubt it, since a lot of them were buried in the dump of the overburden. But with a little bit of luck, eventually, we may be able to convince them otherwise.

Mist photograph taken in the Old North Hibbing Cemetery that some believe looks like an angel. *Photo taken by Rhonda Leffler*

Small ectoplasmic mist captured in the Old North Hibbing Cemetery during an investigation. *Photo taken by Brian Leffler*

Chapter Five
The Chase on the Lake

Before we can talk about the Chase on the Lake Hotel, we must first talk about the establishment of the village of Walker. It was incorporated into a village in the late 1800s with many businesses and services established. The main industry in the area was timber, thus meaning that timber men from all over would be staying in the area so that they could work. The natural types of businesses flourishing were the saloons and hotels. Several of the prominent hotels in Walker at the time were the Bush, Spencer, Waldorf, Columbian, Spaulding, and the Pameda.

The Pameda was located in the Ellis Building and is the one that we are most concerned with in this story. P. H. McGarry owned the Pameda. In 1894, a man by the name of L. W. Chase came from Brainerd to Walker and rented the barroom in the hotel. In 1896, Mrs. Chase and their two daughters, Isabel and Edna, came to Walker and even lived in a tent on the shores of Leech Lake. In 1898, the Chase family purchased the Pameda and changed the name to The Chase Hotel.

In 1899, one Colonel J. S. Cooper and "party" met at the Chase Hotel. They discussed a new plan for a national park to be placed in the region of the headwaters of the Mississippi River and to include Lake Itasca, Lake Winnibigoshish, Cass Lake, and Leech Lake. They continued this operation for many years, and in 1915, they decided to invest in further construction. On the site where Mrs. Chase and their daughters lived in the tent, they decided that a new lodge would be placed. They completed construction and named the new lodge the Isabel Annex. The brochures of the time stated that it had twenty rooms and a ballroom. This was the site of many conventions and various entertaining evenings out for people.

Just prior to the grand opening of the New Chase Hotel, tragedy struck the Chase family. Lorin W. Chase, the only son of Mr. and Mrs. L. W. Chase died quite suddenly from complications of pneumonia. Lorin was a very young twenty-two years of age. He was being set up to be the manager of the New Chase Hotel and was the new up-and-coming member of the "younger set."

The date was Thursday June 8, 1922, and the extravaganza that welcomed The New Chase into public use was the most extravagant ever seen in the village of Walker at the time. The management of The New Chase spared no effort or expense in preparation for the grand opening of the new hotel. The celebration was held at 8:00 pm on this particular Thursday with music provided by the famous Dot Van Orchestra, as well as a banquet for guests of the opening. Simultaneously, there was dancing to the orchestra music.

The front of The Chase on the Lake building as it appeared in the spring of 2006.
Photo taken by Brian Leffler

At 9:30 pm Mr. G. A. Kulander, the toastmaster of the ceremony, introduced Mayor Wilcox for the opening address, after which Judge Stanton from Bemidji gave the main talk of the evening. Following the main talk were short addresses by some high-powered state representatives, namely Senator McGarry, Representative DeLurry and Mr. E. I. P. Staede. There were many vocal arrangements performed by one Miss Burke, and speakers were sprinkled throughout the presentation at just the right intervals to keep everyone interested. A joyous time was evidently had by all and was talked about for a very long time afterward. The New Chase was booked to capacity immediately after opening and kept being booked solid for a length period of time. After all, she was the grand lady of the village of Walker.

July 1st of 1923 saw the grand opening of a new attraction on the beach in front of Isabel's, which was, of course, right next to The New Chase. This attraction was the newly invented Sellner Slide, which was beginning to pop up around amusement parks and fairs nationwide. It was basically a sloping ramp that utilized a water toboggan with ball bearing wheels that would get moving quickly as individuals would ride the toboggans into the water. It really does look like a lot of fun, and I am guessing that there were many youngsters who had countless hours of laughs riding this new-fangled invention.

The New Chase Hotel was never one to stand still for very long, at least where innovation and updating was concerned. The first renovation took place only five years after the doors opened. The old dining room became a dance hall as the Cass County Pioneer Newspaper declared on May 20, 1927.

Speak Very Easy at This Hotel...

During the time of prohibition, people around the country were still obtaining alcohol and drinking as if there were no laws against it. The only difference was that they had to do it in secret locations to keep the police off of their backs. This was when the nation saw the birth of the speakeasy. Tiny rooms were placed out of the way, where people could drink and not get arrested—well, as long as they didn't get caught, anyway.

The police would often raid establishments that were thought to have a speakeasy located inside, but it always seemed that there was a tip to the owners and everything was in its place and hidden by the time the police came knocking on the door. It would almost seem that the police went through the motions, probably enjoying the speakeasy as much as everyone else and not really wanting to catch the people, nor shut down the illegal bar.

The New Chase was no exception. The speakeasy was located in the corner of the basement and came complete with a bar, stools, and chutes to supply the bartender with booze to serve. It was a very ingenious set-up and went for many years without being shut down. This speakeasy is a very tiny little room, though, and would only service a very few customers at any one time.

This was also the era of slot machines and gambling. In July of 1929, the Cass County Sheriff ordered all establishments to pull their slot machines out, but it didn't take long before they were right back in the stores, bars, and hotels. By the early 1930s, The Chase had four or five slot machines operating in the hotel. Manager Finnegan had once stated that the profit from these machines was almost enough to pay for the heating bill at The Chase for the entire winter. This was a very lucrative business to say the least. The Chase Hotel placed each of their machines in a large metal cabinet on wheels. When the police raids were eminent, and usually well known to the management, the cabinets were rolled into the private sleeping rooms on the first floor of the hotel where police would never look. They kept this up for quite some time until just before World War II began. It was at that time that the government slapped a $50 tax on all machines. The list from the manufacturer provided the government with who owned the machines, and since The Chase didn't want to pay this tax to have the machines on their property, they got rid of them, finally bringing an abrupt end to a long profitable era.

Sunday, July 17, 1938, was a day of mourning for the village of Walker. This was the day that Lawrence Woodruff Chase died. He died of throat cancer and had done battle with it for seven years. He fought hard, but after a five-hour hemorrhage, he lost the battle and died. His death took place at about three or four in the morning. There are two different accounts, in two independent newspapers, that each give a different time. He was seventy-six years old at the time of his death, and he did die inside The Chase Hotel itself. Laid to rest on Wednesday, July 20, 1938, scores of people from the entire region turned out to pay their respects to L. W. Chase. Reverend William E. Hammond conducted the funeral services at the Evergreen Cemetery.

Chase's early childhood was spent in New York State, but he moved to Chippewa Falls and Eau Claire, Wisconsin as a younger man. He married Louise Hanson on January 2, 1887, in a place called Kilbourne City. You may have heard of this place, but most likely by its new, more famous name—Wisconsin Dells. They remained here for only a short period before moving on to Ashland, Wisconsin and then on to Brainerd, Minnesota in the year 1889.

Chase was engaged in business in Brainerd for several years, until finally moving to Walker in 1894. The railroad had not yet reached Walker when he moved to the area, but was finally built in the year 1896. Walker was a very rugged, wild logging community at the time he moved to the region. His death left a gaping hole in the community as he was one of the earliest settlers in the region and contributed greatly to the building of the community.

Yet another notable death that took place in The New Chase Hotel: Miss Isabel Katharine Finnegan, age 19 on Sunday, September 13, 1936. She was born in Walker on February 28, 1917, and attended the Walker School for a brief period before resuming her studies in Minneapolis, Minnesota at St. Stevens. She then moved on to Central High School until June of 1936, when she graduated. While she attended Central High School, she was chosen to be a member of the National Honor Society as well as being the Club Editor of the Central High Newspaper. She continued to live in Minneapolis, but visited the Walker area as often as possible to visit with her many friends who noted her wonderful, loving personality that was the envy of all who knew her.

Miss Finnegan had been dealing with an incurable heart condition for the last two years of her young life. On Saturday, the day before she died, she must have known that death was eminent at that point and went into town to walk among the businesses and meet with all of her friends so that she could say goodbye. This was truly a life cut short, and in typical fashion, the good truly seem to die young.

In the years to come, The New Chase Hotel would change hands many times, the first of which occurred in the year 1946, when the Chase family would give up their reign as the owners of the grand lady, selling the property to one Mr. A. F. Kruse, a restaurant operator from Grand Forks, North Dakota. Mr. Kruse did state that he intended on re-opening the dining room at the hotel.

As I said before, The Chase was not about to stand still. In the late 1950s or early 1960s (the record does not specify), an indoor, covered and heated pool was installed next to the hotel itself. In 1963, the entire lobby was remodeled, and in the year 1964, she underwent some major renovation with the addition of new carpeting, new furniture, suites, and a host of new amenities, such as new mattresses and rugs throughout. The current owners, Mr. and Mrs. Floyd Jones, also stated in 1964, that they had plans to start serving three meals a day at the hotel starting in June of that year.

Things rolled along for The Chase on the Lake Hotel for many years, with different owners taking over the grand hotel and making changes and upgrading. Unfortunately, I never got there to enjoy the supper club that was overlooking the Leech Lake. My mom did, however, and said that she was a beautiful place with very good food. She was lucky enough to enjoy The Chase while operational in the early 1980s.

The End of a Landmark Era

In 1993, Mark and Katy Schimer purchased the hotel with the intention of restoring it to the grand beauty that it was in years before. They had even submitted plans to the city of Walker to have it done under a tax increment plan. They ran the hotel with the help of their four children right up until Sunday, June 29, 1997, when tragedy struck the grand lady. Fire broke out.

It would seem that nearly the entire town of Walker turned out to watch the firefighters fight the blaze that was suddenly engulfing the historic landmark. Renee Geving of the Cass County Historical Society located in Walker told reporters, "This place had a great impact on early tourism here," and, "The Chase is what really kept tourism here." The Fire Chief at the time, Jan Vanvickle, told reporters that the fire started at about 4:45 pm in a small coffee service area that was located adjacent to the main kitchen. With no sprinkler system in the old hotel, it charred about a third of the building. It was also reported that there was extensive smoke damage throughout the hotel. Even though this much of the building was charred, surprisingly there was no real structural damage to the building—though the blaze was fought for over two hours before it was finally considered under control.

The Shimers watched the historic hotel burn in horror, feeling their dreams of a two million dollar renovation slip away in front of them. They had even re-opened the speakeasy in the basement in an effort to bring her back to her original state. Sadly, the hotel remained unopened and unused from the time of the fire until present day.

In April of 2006, I was attending a medical diver scuba class in Walker for the Itasca County Sheriff's Department. We were there over the weekend. (I am a scuba diver and a member of the Sheriff's Dive Team in that county.) I had gone into a local establishment to get some dinner and relax for a while after the grueling eight-hour class. I was, of course, wearing my hat with the Northern Minnesota Paranormal Investigators logo on it. This had seemed to

break the ice on many conversations. When I wear it, quite often people see me as an advertisement for our group, and they feel comfortable coming over to talk with me and to explain what they have going on in their lives as it relates to the paranormal.

I had finished my dinner and moved up to the bar where I met some local people who asked about my hat, of course, starting the conversation off. They asked me about the ghost symbol on the background of the state of Minnesota emblem along with the N.M.P.I. embroidered on it meant. They then began to show me some photos that they had taken that they thought were paranormal in nature. One of the photos was one taken at another bar in Walker and showed a very dark setting with some streaking, colored lights. They showed me several pictures that looked the same way and they asked me to "look at my ghost!"

Well, I didn't want to dash their hopes, but I am afraid I had no choice but to explain the truth behind their pictures. You see, these pictures were taken on a digital camera in a low light setting that makes a steady picture virtually impossible to accomplish. What I had to tell them was that because they were in a low-light setting, they had what is known as *motion blur*. It is a very common occurrence in photography and especially with digital cameras. With the dark setting of the bar, the open "shutter" time is elongated, and since digital cameras are so silent when taking a picture, they often have not completed their process when the photographer moves the camera. This usually happens at the last possible fraction of a second, and the motion blur only happens to the brightest objects in the picture—in this case, the neon signs hanging on the walls of the bar.

They were, of course, disappointed, but they suggested that I talk with their friend, Eddy, about The Chase on the Lake Hotel there in Walker. They contacted Eddy and explained to him who I was and that I was a paranormal investigator. Eddy came over to me a few minutes later and began to tell me about The Chase and its weird happenings.

Eddy explained to me that he was from California and had recently moved to Minnesota at the behest of Jarrod, the current owner's son. It would seem that Jarrod wanted to give Eddy a job working as a cook, as well as to help to "gut" the inside of The Chase for its new twelve million dollar renovation that would begin to restore her to her original appearance and functionality.

Eddy told me, that night, many tales of weird things happening to both him and Jarrod while in the hotel working on the renovation process. He told me of the "creepy" feeling of being watched from the very first time he entered the old building. He went on to tell me that he would also hear doors slamming and footsteps on the floor above him with nobody else in the building, and the doors all locked to prevent anyone from coming in.

It was also explained that when they would work on the hotel at night, and when it was time to leave, they would shut off the lights and run for the door as fast as they could without looking back at all. Eddy was scared to death of the place. Jarrod was a little bit tougher when it came to being afraid of the paranormal. He is a non-believer in ghosts and doesn't buy into it at all, but even with this attitude, he would still find himself running out of the building at night once the lights were turned off.

The Investigation

When our team arrived at the hotel in the spring, it was still very cold outside with a low at about the thirty-eight degree mark. Of course, the hotel is pretty much disconnected from the world since the fire, having never been purchased or renovated until 2006. We met with Eddy and Jarrod who gave us access to the building and then a little tour while it was still daylight. They showed us many hazardous areas to watch out for, such as opening a door marked "phone" and finding a small phone-booth-sized room that had no floor—you can see directly into the basement. There are also many other places in the old hotel that are just as dangerous, with pieces of flooring missing as well as weak floors that sound as though they will give way at any time. (If anyone plans on conducting an investigation in such a hazardous location, please heed all safety precautions. Not everthing dangerous is ghost related, and there are many things in some locations that will injure or even cause death.)

Other than being in a state of disarray, the lobby appeared fairly normal. When we walked down the hallway toward the backside of the building that faced the lake, we discovered the ravages of the fire that tore through the building. We could see scorched walls and doors, as well as missing walls and areas of floor. We were also able to still smell the smoke of the fire, even after approximately thirteen years had passed since that terrible day. During our tour, while on the third floor, we had all passed one of the many guest room doors that stood open. As soon as we passed, the door slammed shut. We opened the door and were unable to get the door to slam shut in the same manner again.

Was it paranormal? I don't know for sure—it could have been related to the wind since there were many windows on that floor. We didn't, however, change anything when we went up to this floor. The windows had been open for a very long time, as well as the door itself. Why did it wait until our group passed the doorway before it decided to slam shut? It was a very strange experience but, of course, not proof of the paranormal.

We proceeded to learn the location of the speakeasy and even took a very creepy tour of the boiler room sitting down in what I can only describe as a "pit" located behind a heavy steel door. It comes complete with a rickety wooden set of steps leading downward. We decided that we would run off into town after this tour and have some dinner to discuss just exactly how we would set up our equipment to attempt to capture as much paranormal evidence as we possibly could.

Once the sun set, we returned to the hotel and began setting up the equipment for our long, cold night's investigation. We placed a security camera on the second floor looking down the hallway, while placing another one in the basement at the end where the fire had started. We also placed our camcorder in infrared mode on a tripod and let it record directly into the speakeasy.

While setting up the cameras, we were able to capture an EVP that struck me as very odd. It was while we were setting up the security camera on the second floor, that I recorded something that sounded like some sort of chant in a foreign language. It was an EVP that really raised the hairs on the back of my neck the first time I had heard it play on the tape. To this day, I have been unable to identify exactly what it is that is being said on the tape, but it does sound almost like a spell being cast. Could this be what it was?

We then began to walk around within the scorched walls of the hotel. We were talking with the spirits and hoping that we would capture their answers on audiotape creating some fantastic EVP for us to help prove the haunting that we had heard about. Of course, we were completely unaware that we had already captured one of the strangest ones we would ever hear.

While investigating the third floor, Kyle, another investigator (unnamed), and myself were exploring the dark rooms and trying to make contact when the other investigator heard a male whisper in her ear and felt breath on her neck. This voice made her feel very uncomfortable, and she even felt a little bit threatened. This was the first of a long list of paranormal encounters that our team would have this night. Of course, we didn't know it yet, but the three of us had had an encounter on the third floor when we were discussing the next location of our security camera which was sitting on the second floor in the hallway. We were asking each other where it should be moved, when a diminutive, yet very clear voice chimed in and said "down in the basement," offering us this as a recommendation for the next location of the camera. The most interesting part of the EVP I recorded was that it was only recorded on *my* tape recorder. Both Kyle and the other investigator had their recorders going at the same time, and we were standing within two feet of each other, yet it did not appear on either of their tapes. It only appeared on mine.

It is my belief that this EVP was imprinted directly onto the magnetic tape and not an audible sound. If it were an audible sound, it would have been recorded by all three recorders simultaneously and not only on one tape. This voice is very clear on the tape and is considered a *Class A* EVP. Unbeknownst to us at the time, there was also a very strange phenomena going on in the basement on one of the security cameras. A black cat had apparently wandered into the basement, noticed the infrared emitters on the camera, and sat down to check it out for a minute before getting back up again and heading toward the original kitchen. Why is that interesting at all you ask? Well, this cat had no apparent means of entry into the building and was never seen before or after by anyone at the hotel that I have heard. It also didn't have a reflection in the eyes from the infrared emitters. When anyone is in front of a camera in infrared mode their eyes shine very brightly in most cases. Cats especially, while in the dark, will have what looks like headlights on the front of their faces. We found it absolutely amazing that this cat didn't have any reflection at all.

It wasn't very long into the investigation when Kyle and myself wandered into the basement to do some exploring. Our first strange encounter there was that of a man that Kyle sensed was watching us. The very odd thing about this encounter was that I could smell grease—you know, the type that you associate with the lubrication of bearings and machinery. It was a kind of stale smell that seemed to permeate the very fabric of the man's clothing as he followed us around in the dark and very creepy basement.

In the end, our group wound up recording several wonderful videos as well as a multitude of EVPs. This grand old hotel was one of the most fantastic investigations that our team has ever taken on. It was chocked full of paranormal experiences that put all of us in a very heightened state of awareness yet left every one of our spirits feeling quite drained and satisfied at the same time. We finally pulled away from the hotel at about two in the morning, feeling chilled to the bone from the cold, but satisfied that we had walked into a very haunted location, met the challenge head on, and made many contacts with the spirits of the people that once had very strong ties with The Chase on the Lake Hotel.

This is how the lobby appears as of the spring of 2006. The once Grand Lady is in a shambles since the fire that decimated it thirteen years ago. *Photo taken by Brian Leffler*

The back stair area that took the brunt of the damage in the fire
that occurred thirteen years ago. *Photo taken by Brian Leffler*

Chapter Six
Union Depot

The Duluth Union Depot & Transfer Company was first established in the year 1889. It was put together in order to acquire the land and begin construction of a union passenger station, as well as the station to be utilized as a transfer station for all railroads entering or departing the city of Duluth. The Union Depot began construction in 1890. It was completed in March of 1892, costing a whopping $615,027. Some of the railroads to use the facility were Northern Pacific, Soo Line, and the St. Paul & Duluth.

The Union Depot as it appears in the late winter of 2006.
Photo taken by Brian Leffler

During the heyday years of the Depot, 1910 to 1920, the facility handled upwards of fifty trains a day. The Union Depot finally saw its commercial train business cease after a very long time and shut down in 1969, where it sat idle for several years and was slated for destruction. It was saved from the scrap heap by being designated a national historic site in 1971.

This building is very unique in design. The famous Boston Company Peabody, Stearns and Furber designed it. The Union Depot is one of the finest examples of French Norman architecture this country has ever seen. It is reported that Robert Peabody himself designed it, and it was patterned after an existing building in eastern Canada. The building is almost medieval in design with its turrets and large roof proportions.

Although the design of this building is beautiful, progress cannot be stopped. It has undergone several renovations and modifications to suit the needs of the time. The first of these took place in 1924, when the large train shed was removed and replaced with smaller "butterfly" sheds instead. This was done at a cost of about $100,000. The next renovation took place in the year 1945, when the grand vaulted ceiling of the waiting room, now known as the Great Hall, had a false ceiling installed. After being tagged a National Historic Site in 1971, it was decided that the building should undergo another renovation and be brought back to its original splendor, remaining available for people to visit and enjoy.

This marked the beginning of the Cultural Center of Duluth which evolved into The St. Louis County Heritage and Arts Center's Historic Union Depot. It is still nicknamed "The Depot," though, since its other name is quite a mouth full! During this two million dollar renovation, the false ceiling was removed exposing the large wood beam construction of the roof. There is a huge train museum, a children's museum, art gallery, and the theater which is home to five different performing arts organizations. The Depot has become one of the city's most identifiable landmarks.

During the long life of the Depot as a train station, it not only saw trains affiliated with industry, but also passengers. Duluth was the main hub for immigrants coming into America and moving toward the west. Countless numbers of immigrants spent time in the Depot. They would come directly from New York's Ellis Island. Many of them would then either go further west, or end up in Minnesota's Iron Range where they would set up their lives as mine workers to start and support their families. This connection is why I believe that there is ghostly activity at the Depot.

You see, as I mentioned prior, I don't believe that there has to be tragedy at a location for there to be ghostly activity. I believe that ghosts have the ability to cross over into our world whenever they want to and for any reason they choose. I think that there is a lot of love for the depot. Perhaps they are still there because this was their real first taste of America. I also believe that the builders may be there, because they took real pride in the building and what they were accomplishing. Any of these reasons could explain why there are ghosts at the Depot, and I am only speculating about these reasons. I can assure you, though, that the Depot is haunted.

Setting up our investigation of the Depot began because of my contribution to another book on the paranormal. I was contacted by its author, Hugh Bishop, and asked to contribute some photos and an interview. During our conversation he asked, "Where would your dream investigation be?" I told him, of course, that my dream investigation would be at Alcatraz, locked in there for the entire weekend doing nothing but investigating. He then narrowed his question to a more local scope, and I replied, "Glensheen Mansion." We both knew this would most likely be out of the question, since they won't recognize ghosts in any way. So we dropped down to alternatives. One of those alternative investigations would be the Depot. He told me that he knew the Executive Director, Ken Buehler, and he would probably jump at the chance to have it professionally investigated. I decided to give Ken a call and see if he would allow it. To my surprise, he accepted my invitation to come and investigate.

During the time I talked with Ken, he relayed some stories to me that I found very interesting. One of those stories involved the Northland car that sits in the museum to this day, being taken out and run on the tracks a couple of times a year. This car belonged to then President of the Burlington Northern Railroad, James J. Hill, and was the very first all-steel railcar ever built. It was unbelievable for someone to want an all-steel car in those days; traditionally they were steel frames and chassis with a wooden frame box placed on top. Although expensive and ugly as anything when it was delivered, it was soon transformed into a thing of beauty that served many high-class people.

This car, upon its arrival, was battleship gray and looked like a large tin can. Artisans were put to work on making it what it is today. It took these artisans over a year of painting the steel walls to make it look like a very luxurious and highly polished wood. They accomplished this task using only turkey feathers. The car was the prize of the fleet, so to speak. It was beautiful, and when businessmen from other states would come aboard to attend the annual deer hunt, there was a lot of fun to be had.

You see, there was a freezer on board and it would be full of deer before the businessmen actually arrived on board. Then the train would leave the Depot and begin its trip around the northeastern corner of the state, known as the "arrowhead."

This is where hundreds of logging camps were set up to kick-start the logging industry. They ran the logs down stream on the many rivers that fed Lake Superior and then right to sawmills located in both Duluth, Minnesota and Superior, Wisconsin. These businessmen took these trips to inspect the logging camps and deer hunt. Since the deer hunt was taken care of by an employee filling the freezer, they didn't have to worry about actually shooting any deer. They just brought their rifles and took a photo by a deer so that the wife back home would not get suspicious about the trip. Then they would visit every logging camp, and where there were loggers, there were prostitutes servicing the loggers. They spent their time moving from camp to camp having their way with the ladies of the evening, but when they returned home to the waiting wife, they brought venison and photos of them with the deer. Nobody was ever the wiser.

The Investigation

Our investigation took place on February 19th of 2006. We had done our research and heard the legends about the deer hunters, and were ready to investigate the place that we had heard so much about. We were excited about it, too! Entering the Union Depot, we began to set up equipment. We placed a security camera overlooking the Great Hall, which was originally the waiting area and is host to artwork and artifacts that are on display. We then set up the camcorder with infrared capabilities on the now infamous (to us at least) Northland car. Tape recorders were placed on other train cars, such as the China car, the Snowplow and the Mail car. Then our investigation started with a ritual of walking around with our still cameras—35mm, auto advance, and 400-speed film—as no digital cameras are allowed in our investigations. We each were carrying our other gadgets—like infrared thermometers, full-size tape recorders, and our own personal psychic feelings.

The Northern Minnesota Paranormal Investigators have three really good psychics on the team but two were actually working together that night, feeding off of each other's abilities. Christy Sandnas and Rhonda Leffler were seeing everything from dark shadows moving around and following us, to a meeting with a banker, lawyer, and a doctor or two in the boardroom upstairs. (They really enjoyed the meeting the most, I think, out of the entire night.) The conversation went on for quite some time before the meeting adjourned and they no longer were able to see the people sitting at the long table in the center of the room.

Christie reported many ghosts that night to Sheila, who was our newest member and on her first investigation with the team. She reported, at one point, a man following her in a long black coat. I just couldn't resist and had to make a little joke that it was Ken. He was, of course, wearing a long black leather trench coat.

Another one of the tools we use in our investigations, as a guide to get more specific information, is the pendulum. We decided that it would be a good idea to try to make some contact with the spirits there, and we wanted to get some footage of us using it for a local-access television show that we'd put together in Hibbing. Starting to use the pendulum, Phil began recording with a camcorder we'd borrowed from the television channel. We ended up getting just a little over a minute of video with a four-hour battery that was just charged. A spirit was sucking the battery dry! Phil could literally watch the battery indicator on the camera drain during that minute. It was the fastest drain of a battery I had ever seen in all my years of doing paranormal investigations.

We wrapped up the investigation about 1:00 am and headed for home, which was about an hour and a half away. We were both excited to pour over the evidence we had just collected though we were physically drained. The next day, I jumped out of bed and literally raced downstairs where I have my VCR and television hooked up for viewing video captured on an investigation. I watched with anticipation just knowing that something had to have been captured on the previous night's journey. I watched and watched for hours, but not much that was overly exciting could be seen until the very last half hour or so of the tape, recorded by the camcorder on the Northland car. We owe that last half hour of fantastic video to Rhonda. If were not for her turning the camera around 180 degrees, we would have never seen two of the three videos we recorded that night which proved to be very important and groundbreaking.

The first of the three videos we recorded was one that has proven my theory on orbs. I know what you are thinking, "orbs just aren't that great for evidence." Well, I beg to differ. I think orbs are the foundation of paranormal activity. It is my contention that orbs, paranormal ones of course, are the basic essence of the spirit. This building block is where ghosts start, and by utilizing gathered energy, they can manifest into shadow and apparition form. In this first video, I could clearly see an orb move into the center of the shot from left to right. It immediately manifested into a shadow that stood a little shy of six feet tall. We know this because Ken Buehler walked directly through this exact area about five minutes prior to us capturing this video, giving us a comparison of height.

The next amazing video we captured happened only about two minutes after the orb manifested into the shadow. This one was a very bright orb that moved upward directly toward a steel plate on the side of a huge locomotive. The funny thing about seeing this orb though was that it actually gave off its own light that was actually bright enough to cast its own reflection in the dull black steel. It moved closer and closer to the steel of the locomotive until it finally popped through the steel plate and vanished from sight. I could see that the orb itself and the reflection it gave in the steel get closer and closer together, showing that it was moving ever closer to the steel before it disappeared.

There is a huge controversy over whether or not orbs are the genuine paranormal article or not, but this video really helped cement the theory that they are directly related to the paranormal. After all, do any of us really believe that a piece of dust can penetrate a steel plate?

The third and final fantastic video was that of an apparition. This apparition appeared just outside the Northland car. We moved the camera into the interior of the car and decided to film the dining room while we took our team photos (see our website to view them). We had our entire group together outside the car. Unknown to us, there was more activity going on outside the car behind us. The camera captured all of the action. What looked like the top of someone's head, from about the ears up, moved across the right hand side window to the center divider. It then began to move across the left hand window from the center divider to the left hand edge, disappearing from view for a short time. There was a huge difference this time though; the apparition appeared taller now. It was now showing from the shoulders up! It moved back again across this window toward the center divider again and paused. Then it moved to the left hand window for a final time, pausing in the center of that window and then finally started to glow white, turn back into an orb and jet off to the left. All of these fantastic videos are available for your viewing at our website which is located at www.hauntingresearch.com.

Although we captured three fantastic and ground breaking videos in a matter of only about half an hour, we don't believe that we caught many ghosts. We believe that it was possibly one ghost that was moving along with the team and checking us out. You see, this is the first time that the Depot in Duluth has ever had a paranormal investigation conducted. It is my belief that there are ghosts there that are very curious about all of the activity of the living. We weren't there to look at their trains, but to look for them. They probably thought that this was a very strange thing and it was very unfamiliar territory to them. Although I believe that we captured one ghost several times, it doesn't mean that there aren't many ghosts haunting the Depot. It is a very mysterious and wonderful place, non only for the history of our great land, but also as a stockpile of paranormal activity.

This is an orb that was captured in the Great Hall of the Union Depot during our investigation in February of 2006. *Photo taken by Kyle Bruzenak*

Chapter Seven

A Famous Ghost

As you already know, Minnesota has been the home of numerous immigrants. Many of these people came to our state because the climate was so similar to what they were accustomed to experiencing. They came; they worked very hard, and built much of this state's living communities we see today. Grand Marais is no exception to this, and it leads us to the next very interesting investigation for our team.

Matthias Johanesen, as he was known in Oslo, or Matt Johnson, as he came to be known upon arriving in the United States, had a wife, Christina, an eldest son named John, a daughter named Mary, and two younger sons named Chris and Matt. Matthias spent his first summer here in 1887 working on the *David Bowes*, a large sailing vessel that hauled freight and a few occasional passengers.

Jane Ranum's house in Grand Marais as it looked during our investigation in June of 2006. *Photo taken by Brian Leffler*

Matthias also immediately filed a homestead claim located in Good Harbor Hill which lies about six miles from Grand Marais. He had built a log cabin on the property. Eldest son John was the first to arrive in this country behind Matthias. He worked on a racing sailboat owned by an Englishman who sold it to someone in the United States. John had only a train ride before him to Duluth to meet his father.

It wasn't long until Matthias had enough money to buy tickets for his family to come to the U.S. He gave Christina instructions to sell all of their property in Oslo and to come over. The family arrived in New York aboard the steamer *Iceland* in 1888. They left New York by train to Duluth where the family was once again reunited. Matthias and the family stayed in Duluth for a while, as he had begun working in construction on a new elevator. This endeavor ended abruptly, though, as a depression began under the Cleveland administration. For a cost of $3.00 each, the family hitched a ride aboard the *America* from Duluth back up the north shore to Grand Marais. They were even able to bring along the skiff that Matthias had built during his winter alone. The plans were for them to row about five more miles from Grand Marais to Good Harbor Bay and then walk two miles up the hill to the homestead where the cabin now sits.

Upon the arrival of the family in Grand Marais, a nor'easter rolled in and prevented the family from rowing the skiff up to Good Harbor Bay. They were lucky that Matthias had made a friend by the name of Jim Morrison, a full-blooded Chippewa Indian who insisted upon the family staying at his house in town. Matthias had previous dealing's with Mr. Morrison, as he was the one that surveyed his land for him. The family took him up on his offer, and it turned out to be three days before the winds let up enough for them to get out on Lake Superior.

It wasn't too long before Matthias began fishing for a living. Lake Superior was very plentiful for lake trout in those days, and they were selling for about eight cents per pound. Matthias also tried his hand at farming, but soon realized that with such a short growing season and rocky, poor soil, that is wasn't the best way to make a living. The family did have plenty of wild game for meat, so they knew they wouldn't go hungry.

Late in the summer of 1890, Mr. Morrison came by asking to see the homestead paperwork of Matthias' only to discover that he had built his beloved cabin on land belonging to someone else. He was forced to move about a mile away to their rightfully claimed land, so that fall, Christina, Mary, and Matt headed back to Duluth so that they could attend school. Matthias, John, and Chris stayed behind and began moving and building on the new site. They put together a cabin with only beds and a stove, which was enough to satisfy the homestead requirements. This land is preserved by the Cook County Historical Society, which has placed a marker there that reads; "Homestead by Matthias Johnson, the first homesteader of Good Harbor Hill."

Christina returned the following spring only to turn around and leave again the following fall, so that the kids could again attend school. Matt, Jr. started back at school in the second grade, and when finished that year, he had completed studies through the fourth grade, as far as his schooling ever went.

Before the return of his family to Grand Marais, Matthias decided that a cabin on the West Bay would be more convenient for the family. With this cabin in place, they could live in it during the summer months and fishing would be easily accessible. In the fall, it would mean rowing all of the household effects back to Good Harbor Bay and carrying them up the hill to the cabin located there to spend the winter months. This twice-a-year migration continued until the year 1899, when Matthias began to buy some lots in the town of Grand Marais for a better arrangement for the family.

In the year 1894, there were two major events that took place for the family. First, their beloved cabin burnt down due to a forest fire that ravaged the area's forests. And second, at age fifteen, young Matt went to work as a typesetter for the newspaper in Grand Marais—then known as the "Cook County Herald." Matt was destined to be a newspaperman even at this early age. Upon his coming to the paper as a "print devil," the paper published an article that commented, "now watch our smoke."

The Johnson family decided that they would re-build their cabin up on the hill. The materials were brought up to Good Harbor Bay by ship, loaded into the skiff that Matthias built, and then carried by hand up the hill two miles to the building site. (It amazes me as to the things people endured in those days.)

In the year 1899, Matthias decided it was time to build a house in town on the east end of a lower lot that he had just purchased. Chris and Matt were able to pitch in $500.00 each, at the same time having a larger house constructed on the same lot, but on the other end. Both houses faced what was then, the main highway. The boys hired the Holte brothers to construct the house—Chris, Hans, and Andrew would do the work. The house was made of hand-hewn tamarack timber that was actually cut from the trees on the hill where the school currently stands. There are several houses that were built during the same time period using the same timbers, as well as the Bethlehem Lutheran Church, which was built in 1902-1903, and is located on the same block and the Johnson family home.

Not long after this time period, the tamarack trees contracted a disease, and from that point on, all lumber had to be shipped from Duluth. On September 18, 1899, Reverend Aschim, then the pastor of the Bethesda Church in Duluth, came up the shore. Families gathered together for services at the Johnson home and these pioneer families organized "The First Norwegian Evangelical Congregation of Grand Marais." This charter membership included eight families and gathered in each family's home until the time that the church was finished construction.

In 1904, the newspaper that young Matt worked for was sold. It was at this time that he moved to Duluth and worked for various companies as a typesetter and where he met Emma Sather. He married Emma in 1906. Emma was the sister of Chris' wife, Kaja. In 1911, Emma died of tuberculosis, leaving Matt with two young daughters, Margaret (age 4) and Mabel (still an infant).

Fortunately, Matt had an opportunity to buy the Grand Marais newspaper and he jumped at the chance. It turned out to be a very good move for him, because his parents could look after his little girls, and the paper was very profitable for him. Unfortunately, the big house was being rented at the time, and he and his little girls were forced to move into the smaller house with his parents.

The year 1912 saw a change in pastors of the church. Reverend Sandeno was called for the position, and both he and his wife, Bertina, were from the southern part of Minnesota. Reverend Sandeno wrote Bertina's sister, Pauline, and explained that they wanted her to move up for the summer to help with their growing family. He also explained that there was a young man with two little girls that she may be interested in. She replied back, "If you have nothing better than that to offer, you can keep him." Evidently, after her arrival, she changed her mind, and in October of 1915, they were married. Matt continued with the newspaper until the year 1920, when his doctor informed him that he had to quit. His health wasn't too good at this point, due to the tuberculosis that he had contracted from his first wife. As his health later improved, he ran for office as Clerk of Court. He was elected and received $85.00 a month in wages. With this significant drop in pay, Matt was forced to dip into the savings to keep his family's head above water. In 1934, while still the Clerk of Court, Matt decided to purchase a grocery store and was helped out by his children, Ted and Mabel.

The Johnson family was always full of fun and activity even though they were continuing to grow through the years. This family was always welcoming newcomers to the area and served them many meals in their home. They were also people who enjoyed Christmas immensely. They always got together on Christmas Eve at grandma and grandpa's house to spend quality family time cooking large meals, exchanging gifts with one another, and, of course, joining in on church services.

Through the generations, this house has changed hands, but it has always been in the hands of family—which is something you don't often see anymore. Today, Kelli is a fifth generation descendant who is most definitely in line to become master of this wonderful old homestead.

My involvement with Jane began in November of 2005. She had sent an email telling me of ghostly happenings in her home, with incidents beginning in September of 2005, and wanted to know if we would be interested in coming to Grand Marais to investigate her ghosts—she was not at all comfortable with ghostly episodes. She had also sent me a photo that she took in the house, but unfortunately, I didn't think it was of paranormal nature.

We continued to talk and I found out about the Mardi-Gras beads that hang on the door to Kelli's room that move without provocation—and at some very strange times. I also found out about a shadow that Kelli saw in her room, which was a frightful experience for her. It moved toward her while in bed, and it blocked out her view of a lava lamp, which she had placed in her room.

As we talked off and on about her haunting, it was discovered in late December that a friend of Jane's, Barry Cowsill, was killed in September of 2005 in New Orleans by Hurricane Katrina. Barry was a singer in the group "The Cowsills," a contemporary pop group I suspect many of you may have heard of. Barry loved Grand Marais and felt comfortable with Jane and his surroundings. It was quite a shock to Jane to find that she had lost her friend in such a tragic way, and even more of a shock that his body was not discovered until late December of 2005 under a pier.

Jane had noted that her paranormal occurrences had not begun until after Hurricane Katrina passed and wondered if it was possible that Barry's spirit would be at her home. I did tell her that it was very possible, as I do not believe that it takes a tragedy for a ghost to hang around. I am also a firm believer that love can be very compelling, and the deeply-rooted love that Barry had for Grand Marais and Jane's house was enough for him to want to be there. Our team finally set out for Grand Marais, which was about a four-hour drive one way for us, in March of 2006, but had to turn back due to an unexpected snow storm making travel dangerous. We weren't able to make a return attempt until July of 2006.

We arrived at Jane's lovely home in the evening of June 8th. We were very happy that we had finally made it to the house after so much time and hearing about all that had been occurring there over the months. Since there was such a short duration of activity involved with this home, there really isn't any legend or lore surrounding it. We took a quick tour of the home to get our bearings and to decide where the hottest spots were located so that we could set up our equipment. Soon the equipment was set and we were rolling tape, taking pictures, and officially investigating the haunting that I'd heard so much about.

Early in the investigation, Kyle and I were standing in the master bedroom when Kyle suddenly blurted out the name "Sam." He told me that he wasn't sure whether or not "Sam" was a male or female, but he kept getting the name nonetheless. We continued on and I didn't give much thought to the name after that—for probably about an hour or so. Then, while taking a break with Jane outside the house, I asked her, "Does the name Sam mean anything to you?" Her reply seemed to almost stick in her throat as she told me that Sam was the name of her dog that she'd loved for seventeen years. She told me that Sam was "like a child" to her.

He would never run off from her and would play hide and seek in the house with her. It turned out that Sam was a male dog that had been neutered, and I believe this is why Kyle had so much difficulty in determining whether or not Sam was male or female.

It wasn't long after resolving the Sam issue that Christy, a lead investigator and psychic, told Jane that there was "someone sick in the house." She picked up that this sick person was an old lady. She kept getting the name "Paula" in her visions of this woman. (It was very uncanny how accurate both Christy and Kyle were this night.) When Christy told Jane about "Paula," her jaw nearly dropped to the floor.

It would seem that there was an older lady in the family that did live in the house, as you can see by the historical account you previously read. Only, her name wasn't Paula, it was Pauline Johnson. She was around eighty years old when she died, having gotten very sick and refusing to stay in the hospital once she'd been taken. She was brought home and placed in her bed in a shabby add-on room where she lay until she was about ready to die, refusing the hospital for as long as she could stay conscious.

Once unconscious from a stroke, the family took her to the hospital, which was only a short distance away, where Pauline died. I believe that Pauline's love bound her to the home.

Shortly after being told this information, Jane pulled out a family photo album to show Christy. Again, Jane was astounded when Christy pointed to a picture with several older women shown and said, "There she is, and that's Pauline right there." She had accurately identified the sick older woman upstairs.

The third and final weird occurrence that we endured happened in the basement. The basement was a location in the house where Jane was generally afraid. As a relevant side note, the logos on our investigation shirts have the state stitched in green, with a ghost and N.M.P.I. stitched on top of it in glow-in-the-dark stitching. *Why is this important* you may ask? It is because when Gina, Kyle, and myself were investigating the basement together, we had an experience concerning these logos. They would blank out as we watched them. It was very strange, indeed, how I could be looking at Gina and her logo would disappear and then re-appear as if someone or some thing were passing in front of it. We experienced this phenomena for about fifteen minutes.

After returning upstairs from the basement, Kyle began talking about a name that he had picked up on while down there—the name of "David Jacob." Although he didn't realize it at the time, it was one name—he was slightly confused as to which was the correct name, David or Jacob. After presenting this experience and name to Jane, there was even more confusion as she was unable to make any sense of it at all. It was her daughter Kelli who finally put it together and asked her mother if she remembered David Jacob Fredrickson.

As it turned out, he was an older man who had a lot of "young person" type problems. He was always short on cash and never seemed to have anything to eat. Jane invited him in on a regular basis to feed him, as well as give him assistance in buying gas and paying some bills. A fairly unremarkable life that ended at age sixty-two, but touched the lives of Jane, her family, and the house that sits in Grand Marais. We were able to collect the voice of who we think is David Jacob Fredrickson. We did capture an EVP that says, "Kyle, I don't want to hurt you." We think that, possibly, he felt threatened by Kyle being able to read his name, and we also believe that he is the one responsible for blanking out our logos on our shirts. A photograph taken by Kyle during this same time period that we believe is him.

As for Barry Cowsill, we believe that he is residing in Grand Marais, at least part of the time. I was sitting on a bed in the upstairs and asking if he was there. I heard a voice reply to me, "I'm here." It was a very deep, raspy, and almost wheezy voice that sounded like it was struggling to move air in and out. When I described this voice to Jane, she informed me that Barry was in a car accident some years ago and damaged his larynx by hitting it on the steering wheel, as well as having emphysema from being a two-plus-pack-a-day smoker for a very long time. I think that he loved the place so much that he returned there—well, at least for some off and on visit time. I think that he just wants Jane and Kelli to know that he loves them and thanks them very much for treating him like a regular human being, instead of being star struck and regarding him differently.

Jane's house in Grand Marais didn't provide our group with any evidence that will rock the paranormal world, but it did help us to shed some light on the things happening in her home and to find out just who was lingering within the walls of the great old house with tons of history. I am very much looking forward to a return trip to this house to see if perhaps we can learn even a little bit more.

Ectoplasm circling around Brian Leffler during the investigation of Jane Ranum's home in Grand Marais. *Photo taken by Kyle Bruzenak*

Ectoplasm located in almost the same location as the one circling Brian
Leffler and taken only a minute later. *Photo taken by Kyle Bruzenak*

Chapter Eight
Little Swan Cemetery

The Little Swan Cemetery is a very small one. In fact, one of the smallest I have ever been to. It only encompasses a single acre and is now located within the town of Hibbing, but still remains "out in the woods." It started out as a private family cemetery with its very first burials occurring in 1909 and 1910.

On January 22, 1911, an organization by the name of the Little Swan River Cemetery Association was formed. They purchased the land for the cemetery for a whopping ten dollars. This organization has very sketchy beginnings at best. There are no real records of any meetings that still exist today. There are, however, meeting minutes from a group called the Farmer's Club of Swan River with documents dated January 22, 1911 through June 29, 1913. The ledger of the Farmer's Club does list monies taken in and spent, owners of particular lots and burials, the deed for the land itself, and burial certificates. These records are written in Finnish, and once translated, show that there were previous meetings, but no existing minutes from any of these meetings. Nobody is exactly sure as to when the Little Swan River Association dissolved, or for that matter, why. It is believed that the deaths of the original members of the association are speculated to be the reason it fell apart and dissolved. This dissolution has been the cause of the records being passed from one group to the next and for them being incomplete. The cemetery land itself has been passed around also. In the beginning, the cemetery was part of the Lavell Township. Around the year 1918, it became part of the Stuntz Township, and finally about fifteen years ago, became part of the town of Hibbing.

The Little Swan Cemetery is full of legend and lore. It has been a primary site of many amateur "ghost hunters" over the years. There have been accounts of things happening to these ghost hunters out there.

It would seem that a group went out to investigate the cemetery, but they also brought along a skeptic who was not very respectful of the dead. He was making jokes, laughing at what the others were trying to do in order to document the paranormal. He got a little more than he bargained for in the end. He laid down in an indentation in the ground near a tombstone. This indentation was approximately two and a half feet across by about four and a half feet long. Once he did this, he stated that it felt like lying in a freezer. It was unbearably cold and he began having difficulty breathing. This incident caused the group to want to vacate the premises and return home very quickly, as they could not explain it and they were traumatized by it. They returned to their truck and attempted to start it. Of course, just like in all of the horror movies, the truck would not start. While trying over and over to start the truck, they kept hearing footsteps moving closer and closer to their vehicle, but they were unable to see anyone there. Eventually, the truck did start and the terrorized bunch took off from the cemetery and headed home. During their ride home, they were involved in an accident where one of the occupants was thrown from the truck, but luckily not too badly injured.

Some of the people who were in this group decided to make another journey to the cemetery at a later time and again experienced some weird goings on. Yet again, on the way home, they were involved in an accident where another member was ejected from the truck and slightly injured.

Another account places one woman and two men on four-wheelers riding on the small dirt road that passes in front of the cemetery. Their machines were running fine throughout their entire trip—until they passed in front of the cemetery. It was at this point that all three machines shut off and did not want to re-start at all. They tried continuously to start them, but to no avail. During this time, they heard footsteps moving toward them with nobody there. They finally got the machines to start and tore out of the location at a very high rate of speed.

Another account tells of a headstone that was glowing green upon one gentleman's trip to Little Swan. This has been seen on more than one occasion. There must be a light reflecting off the stone, you may think, but there is no electricity at this cemetery. There are no lights, other than the lights you can carry there yourself. Keep in mind that this cemetery is out in the middle of nowhere, sitting at the edge of some farmland and very thick woods.

This same man was out on another occasion with a woman and some other friends. The woman he'd brought along was very disrespectful and conducted herself in a very childish and profane manor. She had been jumping on top of stones and sitting on them as well. She must have sat on the wrong one at some point, because while sitting on it, she was slapped across the face and knocked off of the stone. You guessed it; this was the stone that had been glowing on previous excursions. Several people out there witnessed this slap and she did show a red swollen area on her cheek in the shape of a handprint. On yet another trip made to the cemetery by this man with an infrared video camera, he noticed a man standing at the edge of the woods with something resembling a flashlight in his hand. This could only be seen on the camera and not with the naked eye. He also witnessed several orbs flying around in the cemetery that night on the camera.

When N.M.P.I. made the trek out to this cemetery, we were all very excited after hearing these stories from the people who had scary trips to Little Swan. Our experience was not nearly so harrowing. I did find the indentation in the ground from the story I'd heard, and I laid down in it for about ten minutes. Unfortunately for me, the ground was not unusually cold there. It didn't read as being extra cold at any point during our investigation on the infrared thermometer either.

We were, however, having some strange feelings, and the psychics in our group were picking up on spirits there. My chill was going off quite regularly also. (I should really explain what I am referring to when I say "my chill." It is not like a cold shiver you get when you have been outside too long on a blustery day, but more of a small electrical charge that runs directly, and very quickly, down my spine from the base of my skull to my tail bone. The best description I can give as to what it feels like is the charge you get on your tongue when you place a 9 volt battery on it. That tingle most closely resembles the feeling. Now, when a spirit is touching me, I not only get this chill that runs down my spine, but also a clenching of the jaw, not unlike biting into something sour like a lemon.)

We did see the headstone glowing slightly, and it was a moonless night, which is what I thought might have been the cause of it. It was a very strange sight and only happened with this one particular stone. Nobody made any attempt to sit on the stone—we are not disrespectful toward the dead. (Not that the thought didn't cross my mind, though.)

We did capture one fairly clear EVP that evening. I had asked if I could take their picture, and I did capture a *yes* on audiotape. It did require a little bit of filtering and slowing to make it audible, which did not allow me to call it a *Class A* EVP, but we were able to hear the response quite well enough for our purposes. We also captured a couple of mists on film that night that we could not explain.

All in all, Little Swan Cemetery is one that is shrouded in mystery. We know there are spirits still hanging around out there. We even found a grave belonging to a woman who was on board the *Titanic*, dying on that horrible day. I think that some day when we have time, we will make another trip out to the Little Swan Cemetery and say *hi,* but we will remain respectful of the poor souls buried in this tiny little cemetery in the woods.

Chapter Nine
U. S. S. William A. Irvin

The *William A. Irvin* was built back in 1938 by the American Ship Building Company located in Lorain, Ohio. This ship was used almost exclusively as a carrier of iron ore and limestone, which it hauled for its owners, U.S. Steel's Great Lakes Fleet. It hauled on the Great Lakes for forty years and was the flagship of the fleet.

For those of you who have never been on board a Great Lakes ore ship, let's take a little tour. The tour of the ship is important, as it will help you understand where events have taken place.

The *William A. Irvin* is 610 feet and 9 inches long, 60 feet wide and 32 feet and 6 inches deep. The carrying capacity of the *Irvin* was 14,000 tons. This seems like a lot, but on the average nowadays, ships are carrying twice that amount. When you enter the deck up top at about mid-ship, you are standing on the Spar Deck. There are 18 hatch covers up here that measure 38 feet long by 11 feet wide. These hatches open up into the 3 main cargo holds. There are also railroad tracks on this deck that are painted a brilliant yellow that were used for the hatch crane that was used to lift the hatch covers when they were unclamped. This crane was a necessary tool, as each cover weighs 5 ½ tons each. As you walk around to the rear of the ship, you reach what is known as the fantail. The fantail is where the stern anchor is located. This anchor weighs 6,000 pounds and the 2 anchors at the bow of the ship weigh 8,000 pounds each.

U. S. S. William A. Irvin ore ship sitting docked in Duluth, Minnesota. *Photo taken by Omnimax Theater staff*

Amazingly enough, each link in the chains that tie the anchors to the beautiful ship weighs 40 pounds per link. One thing to keep from tripping over on the fantail is the tiller. This is an alternative method of steering the ship. You see, the winch for the anchor could be connected to the tiller, and by using this winch, you could move the tiller, which would in turn steer by moving the rudder. The fantail is also the storage place of the extra propeller, as it is most difficult to find two ships with the same design—they would carry an extra one and have it installed at a shipyard, should the need ever arise.

Next, let's go down some stairs from the fantail and directly into the unique (at the time) engine room. The *Irvin* was only the third ship ever built with a steam turbine engine that would provide the power to the propeller through a reduction gear. Prior to this method, they had a very large set of pistons that would travel up and down to provide the power. Sitting adjacent to the engine room is boiler room. It is also unique because it has two boilers that have an automatic coal conveyance system. Before this method, you had lots of dirty guys shoveling their hearts out to keep the boilers stoked and keep power delivered to the engines. The power these steam powered turbines produced was about 2,000 horse power and turning at about 5,600 revolutions per minute. This is where the reduction gear played a very important role, as it would reduce those 56 hundred revolutions per minute down to a comfortable 90 revolutions per minute on the propellers. The *Irvin's* speed, although not super fast, was very good for its time. It would travel 12 ½ miles per hour empty and about 11 miles per hour fully loaded.

The engine room is also home to a red light that indicates a boatload of trouble for the crew. This light is for the general alarm, and would mean that the *Irvin* is either on fire or it is in the process of sinking. If the light were to have come on in a long steady flashing manner of at least ten seconds, it would mean that the ship was on fire, but if it came on with seven quick flashes followed by a single long flash, it meant that the crew needed to abandon ship. This is not something a lot of people would necessarily want to do, since the Great Lakes are so cold and the weather can be an absolute beast at times.

Also, toward the stern of the ship is where you would find the officers' dining room. This is a beautiful long oak table and oak chairs in this room, and considering where it is located (on an ore ship), it really is quite striking. It is connected directly to the main galley of the ship where many meals were served. There were typically nine officers on board the ship; The Captain, First, Second and Third mates, Chief Engineer, First Assistant Engineer, two Second Assistant Engineers and one Third Assistant Engineer. Even though there are only nine officers on board the ship, there are fourteen chairs that surround this magnificent table. The reason for this is that, sometimes, the other crewmembers would eat with the officers, and in later years of the ship's career, there would be occasional cadets who would be on board. They, too, would eat at the officers table.

Everyone on board the *Irvin* ate very well. At most meals, there were at least six different choices that could be made from the menu—which, by the way, was written on a chalkboard. Saturday nights always seemed to be steak night, which always gave them a choice of having a T-bone or New York strip steak. There were many other choices for the other nights including hamburgers, roast beef, and the list goes on. Deserts were also present for the meals with such things as ice cream, some sort of pie, and quite often cake. The galley was always open twenty-four hours a day, but was only staffed during the daytime hours. A hungry crewman could come up to the galley any time for a snack if hungry, or eat some of the leftovers from that day's meals.

As we move our tour toward the bow of the ship, we first encounter another dining room. This dining room was meant for the guests on board the *Irvin*. It is decked out very nicely and would be able to make the grade at just about any five-star restaurant. Very nicely adorned in polished wooden walls, fine silverware, crystal glasses, and elegant dining ware, the table even comes complete with a nice brilliant white tablecloth. This dining room was used by guests of U.S. Steel while staying on board, as well as the captain's wife, who would visit usually once or more per year.

As we continue on, we reach the forward superstructure. On the lower two levels of this area two guest rooms are located on each floor. These rooms are actually quite elegant, even more so than anyone would expect on board an ore ship on the Great Lakes. They seem more like they belong on board a grand passenger liner than this type of ship. They come complete with two beds, several portholes, and a simulated fireplace where lights are used instead of flames, so that red light in the engine room doesn't start flashing unnecessarily.

On the second floor there was also a guest lounge. This area had a bar where one could be served drinks. It usually had a card table set up with people playing a game or two. In the latter years of it's operation, the *Irvin* included a twenty-five-inch screen color television, which was quite large at the time. The company did not have stipulations for guests becoming intoxicated while on board, but it certainly did have them for the crew—well, at least a very loose policy. It would seem that the rules for the crew getting intoxicated were considered on an individual basis for each captain and ship.

Now, as we go up another level in the forward superstructure, we enter the pilothouse. This is where all the action took place for navigating the very large ship through what seems like very tight quarters in some of the harbors. This is also where the *Irwin* was lined up at the proper dock to take on or drop off her load of iron ore. When we entered the pilothouse we saw two different steering wheels. One, a large wooden model, as well as a smaller green one. The wooden wheel was used only as a back-up steering wheel, as it was a hydraulic system and very difficult to turn. You had to push hydraulic fluid through six hundred feet of pipe to reach the stern of the ship in order to turn the rudder. The smaller green wheel was the one often used as it is electrically connected to the steering gear in the engine room. It required only electricity, and not manual moving of the hydraulic fluid to move that gargantuan rudder. There is a silver lever next to the green wheel, which is the autopilot. The autopilot is a wonderful system that utilizes the ship's gyroscopes and steering gear, working together to keep the ship on course out in the open lake. The ship also comes equipped with two different compasses. One, the larger of the two, is a gyro-compass which is the main compass used for the navigation of the ship. The second one is a simpler magnetic compass like the ones that we are all familiar with from our scouting days when we were kids. Well, it is a bit larger but works on the same principles.

There are also two radar sets on board. One is the Raytheon Mariner's Pathfinder, which has a maximum range of forty miles, and the Decca radar set, which is the newer one, added in 1966. The Decca has a maximum range of forty-eight miles. Next to one of the doors to the pilothouse, there is a very nifty little gadget called the RDF, or radio direction finder. This unit is a way to find your location and operates on Morse code signals that are put out by lighthouses. By simply tuning into two different Morse code signals, you could plot your position by the location of both lighthouses you have just tuned into.

There you have it. A very abbreviated tour of the ore ship, *William A. Irvin*. Although there is much more to see on board, this should give you a little bit of a general layout of the decks and where things are located. The *William A. Irvin* has not just been a joyous retreat for people and a working ship. It has also been the location of a tragedy.

During the time I spent on the ship after our investigation, doing a couple of local radio shows about the haunting on board, I was told a story by a woman who came to visit us on board during a particular morning show. She told me of a tale of tragedy that occurred early in the ship's life that included the death of her Uncle Jimmy. Jimmy was working on the deck of the *Irvin* when it is suspected that a large gust of wind came along and blew him into the cargo hold. He plunged to the bottom of the empty hold and died immediately from the fall.

This story was quite interesting as it was one that even the staff on board the ship had never heard of. It makes me wonder, though, how many other's died during the building of the ship that we have no idea about? Let's face it, back in those days—the late 1930s—the working conditions were not as good or as safe as you would find today. A shipyard was a very dangerous place to be spending a majority of your waking hours. Unfortunately, the person telling me of her Uncle would not give me his last name, as there were still relatives living who would have a difficult time in thinking that his spirit may still be residing on board.

A much more famous death occurred on the *Irvin* as well. Well, it was more heavily publicized anyway. It seems that back in the mid 1950s, there were three men on duty, watching the boilers and keeping them stoked, when a water tube broke open spraying water on the hot boilers. This created a tremendous amount of steam, which scalded the men inside the boiler room. William Wuori, age fifty-nine from International Falls Minnesota, died from the injuries sustained in the accident while the other two crewmen; Leon Shuffitt, Jr. from Bensonville, Illinois and Stanley Pennell, age forty-three, were in fair condition at a Sault Ste. Marie, Michigan hospital. (Mr. Shuffitt's age was not given in the account of the accident.) This was the horrible tragedy that occurred on the ship's first outing of the season, occurring White Fish Bay, not far from where the fabled Edmond Fitzgerald went to the bottom. I wonder sometimes if there aren't areas like these in the world—loaded with bad vibes, making this sort of tragedy occur more often than in other places in the world.

Our Odyssey on board the *Irvin* began with a phone call. It would seem that the people who run the ship's tours saw a television spot advertising the seminars N.M.P.I. had done at the Depot in Duluth. They called Ken Buehler and then made contact with our group, feeling that it would be a very interesting thing to have a paranormal investigation done on the old ship turned tourist attraction. They told me of strange noises that occurred when nobody else was on the ship with the exception of a maintenance man locking the doors and turning off the lights. These are common occurrences that don't really seem to bother the staff much, as I think they are getting used to having ghosts on board with them. Some of the strange noises they hear are slamming doors, footsteps, and disembodied voices of the dead.

This opportunity sounded way too intriguing to pass up, so we figured out a date to do the investigation and made all of the arrangements so that we could be there long after their normal hours of operation for the tours. We made arrangements to take a preliminary tour of the ship about two weeks prior to actually investigating the ship and found that the logistics of investigating a ship of this size would be difficult at best. There was only one easy way to get from the bow to the stern without traversing many ladders, and that was by using the main deck. It was virtually impossible to set up our home base on the main deck because of being exposed to outside weather conditions, so it was decided to break up the investigation into sections.

We decided that we would set up video cameras in the bow section first while we primarily investigated the mid ship and stern areas first. This would allow us to leave the cameras rolling without any interference from investigators. Then, after a period of time, we would move the cameras to the mid ship area, and finally the stern section. This meant setting up our home base two different times, but it did seem like the only feasible alternative, since there was just too much area to cover all at one time.

We also had to deal with electricity issues such as DC current. We had to be very careful not to plug our equipment into the wrong outlets so that we didn't ruin it. This was the game plan we came up with at our meeting, and we did make sure that when we arrived to investigate, that they had a maintenance staff there to help us out—unlocking doors, granting access to areas that normally are locked and not on the regular tour, and assisting us with the electrical issues.

Upon our arrival at the *Irvin*, we were greeted by the last few remaining tourists who were just leaving the ship, as it was closing time for the tours that day. We proceeded into the gift shop area where the team was supposed to meet and met Bill for the first time. Bill was the maintenance guy who was gracious enough to change his work schedule and accept a shift on a late Saturday night, instead of doing what he normally does on any given Saturday night. Bill was interested in the investigation, though, and even though it was a work shift for him, he still enjoyed seeing how a professional paranormal investigation was carried out from beginning to end. We soon put Bill to work for us by sending him to the bow of the ship to unlock all the doors, so that we could get our cameras set up in that location.

We began the daunting task of carrying tons of equipment from mid ship where the gift shop was located toward the bow section. This meant carrying it up very steep ladders in some locations, and some of those locations are very tight with only enough room for a single person to enter, making it very difficult for that person to carry a large plastic tote full of camera gear into the area. Our team is very persistent, though, and managed to get all of the needed equipment into the bow to begin investigating this wonderful ship.

We placed Kyle's security camera into one of the forward crew's quarters first. This was a location that both Kyle and Christie felt that there was a considerable amount of activity. Next, I set up a security camera in the First Mate's quarters, directly above the area where Kyle was placing his camera. The third security camera stayed at home base in the area of the gift shop. It ended up being placed in a tunnel that ran from the shop toward the front of the ship; there was a locked door at the end which we did not have Bill open.

It didn't take a very long time for us to have the first of many paranormal encounters on board the ship. Kyle's camera was unplugged after only about five minutes of filming, so when we came back to move the camera, we found that he had recorded primarily blue screen, because there was no feed from the camera.

We plugged the camera in again and continued filming in this area for a while with no other incident with the plug. I did move my camera from the First Mate's quarters to that of the Second and Third Mate's quarters and let it run for a while, viewing their old room, located right next to the room where the motors are situated for pulling up and dropping the eight-thousand-pound anchors.

Unfortunately for Kyle and me, we spent a great deal of prime investigating time setting up, disconnecting, and moving cameras. This is a necessary evil during an investigation, but because there is so much territory to explore with these cameras, they had to be moved quite readily to cover as much as possible.

This crew's quarters, where Kyle had initially set up his camera, had an access tunnel running straight away from this room, down the starboard side of the ship just inside the outer hull and just outside the forward cargo hold. It runs just past mid ship, then ends with a door that remained locked during the investigation. This proved to be a very interesting part of the ship that where Christy and Kyle would be able to exercise their psychic abilities quite fully.

Christy picked up on four names that she had mentioned only to Gina while they were spending time down that tunnel trying to make contact. The names were David, James, Sam, and Bill. *Why is this significant?* you may ask. Well, when I was down in the same tunnel with Kyle, about an hour later, he came up with exactly the same four names. When he told Gina about the names he'd heard, she was astounded, because she'd not said anything to anyone else about what she'd gotten. Of course, though psychic impression is never proof of the paranormal to anyone other than the people experiencing it at the time, it was still a very nice confidence builder for our psychics and our team.

There was one point during the investigation that left a couple of the investigators baffled. A door slammed without any explanation or reason near the engine room. It slammed very hard and then popped open again immediately. Though we attempted to re-create this slam many times, the effort was to no avail. Every time the door latched shut and would not pop open again—no matter how hard or soft it was slammed. Again, not proof of paranormal activity, but a very interesting experience to say the least.

The entire team pushed on through the heat for hours, having experiences one right after another and sensing ghostly activity throughout the entire ship—but none seemed more intimidating than the actual boiler room where Mr. Wuori was scalded to death. This room was not very well kept, as it was dirty and littered with debris. The boiler room was the dirtiest location on the ship anyway, even when it was still a working vessel. Now, we have the combination of a dirty room with debris, as well as it being a very dark heart of the ship—with no windows and not much for man-made light sources either. It was truly the bowel of the ship. Then, when you add to the mix the knowledge we had of the man who died in that very location, you have what turns out to be a very creepy area. This boiler room extended upward to three decks with scaffold-type walkways and steep metal-grated stairs. It was usually very dark in this area and made navigating around difficult at best, but also sometimes hazardous.

When all was said and done, the *Irvin* was quite the experience for all involved in this investigation. The evidence stacked up pretty well, too. We captured some pretty good EVP overall. One of the EVP that I captured was recorded on the main deck, port side. The sound was that of an odd growling that appeared twice and then was never heard again. It didn't show up on anyone else's recordings. Another EVP I found quite odd was that of a female voice that says, "Where's your download?" Could this be a more modern day disembodied spirit or perhaps it is a testament that they are able to learn and keep up with the times? You will have to make that decision for yourself. Yet another EVP poses a strange question for us. It states "medical misuse," and what exactly it is referring to is unknown by anyone involved. There were never any reports made, that any of us are aware of, that would tend to make someone think that there were drugs on board for medical purposes that may have been misused in any way, but then again, it is just another piece of the puzzle that perhaps some day will be figured out.

The only video evidence captured by our group during the investigation occurred at the bottom of a flight of stairs in the central cargo hold near the gift shop. I believe that this is the place that Jimmy died. If this is the case, could it be his spirit that we captured on film? What we captured was simple and very difficult to see. It was an energy that flew up very quickly from the bottom center of the screen and then moving at about forty-five degrees to the left. It only appears on two frames of the video and was almost missed when I first viewed it. The second anomaly is also recorded near the same area and looks strikingly similar in form. It is really a non-descript form that is moving very rapidly.

If you are ever in Duluth, Minnesota, feel free to stop by the *William A. Irvin* and take a tour. You never know just what you will find on board this old steam ship. Perhaps you will find more than you bargained for when you pay the fee to get in. You can find information on the ship at www.williamairvin.com.

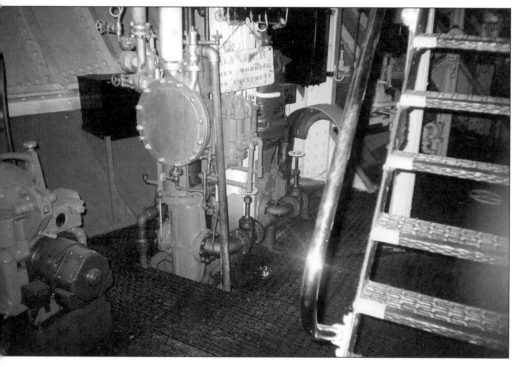

Anomaly captured in the engine room of the *Irvin*. The anomaly is located on the white beam just behind the steps at the top of the picture.
Photo taken by Phil Bodle

Chapter Ten
Linda's House

It was built circa late 1950s on a corner lot in a prime location in the city of Hibbing. It is a straightforward clean-cut house of basic design that looks very unassuming, to be sure. There is more lying under the clean-cut lines of this house though, much more. By the way, Linda is my mother, but her house has been so interesting that I just had to include a chapter on it for this book.

It is difficult to know where to start exactly with this house; there have been so many personal experiences here, that it all seems to get kind of jumbled up. I would guess that Mom's dog, Tova, a very spoiled and bratty Maltese, was one of the first to encounter spirits in the home. She would bark, primarily at night waking Mom up, but what my mom found to be odd is that she was barking from the corner of the bed looking out into the hallway toward the living room—as if someone was there. It was always the same way, too; she doesn't bark toward the windows in her bedroom, just toward the hallway at night. Of course, when the barking first began, my mom would run through the house to see what she was barking at and never did she find anyone or anything that would cause this behavior. She, basically, would wait for her to stop, tell her to hush up, and then they would go back to sleep.

Linda Leffler's house in Hibbing, Minnesota as it appears in the early winter of 2006. *Photo taken by Brian Leffler*

After my mom had been in the house for only a few months, my grandmother from Florida, Edna Coak, came to live with her. She was pushing into her ninety's and was beginning to be unable to live on her own any longer, and instead of placement in a nursing home, she came to live with her daughter in Minnesota. My grandmother was an amazing lady and was always a fixture in my life, even from far away. Thinking back on my earlier childhood memories, she was always "in tune" with her surroundings, and my guess is that she was secretly a little bit on the psychic side.

She had begun to ask my mom about the man who was coming into her room to see her. It was someone that she felt could have been her father or grandfather. She said that the man was very tall, older, with thin dark, short hair. His attire was quite simple; he was wearing cover-alls and work boots. He would come into her room at all hours of the night and wake her up with his presence. Standing over her in the bed for a short period, he would then turn, walk back out of her room and down the hallway disappearing. It still has not been discovered just who the man was in life for sure, but she was pretty convinced that it was one of the two men. For some reason, though, he liked to make himself known to my grandmother on a regular basis.

My grandmother also made mention of a dark figure in the house. This one was wearing a hood and never revealed its identity to her in any way whatsoever. He came only on a couple of occasions and seemed to never scare her. She often said that she felt as if he was there to take her to the other side. She believed very strongly that this was a sign of death.

I was very surprised that this form or the symbolism of death never scared her. I believe that most people would be frightened of such a dark, black entity. I never had the heart to tell her that it was just the way a particular ghost decided to manifest itself to her and really was nothing more than that. Eventually, she no longer saw this figure—after the couple of times that she could recall it. She didn't worry about it much after that, which I believe was a good thing.

My grandmother was convinced that the house was haunted, and it didn't take a lot of convincing for the rest of us, either. She eventually did die in May of 2005, and my mom, Rhonda and I were at her bedside when the moment came for her. I could literally feel myself chill when her spirit finally broke free of the bounds of her broken old body and she was at last free. I certainly hope that she has found peace among those spirits that used to visit her within the walls of my mom's house.

There have been many different experiences in this house for my mom. One of the most common ones deals with the ceiling fan and light above her dining room table. This light has been turning itself on during the middle of the night from about the first week she has owned the house. At first, of course, she thought that she was going crazy and just left it on accidentally, but after getting up and turning it off, it would come back on again. This light does have a remote control to it, and at first I thought that there was perhaps a short in this remote or in its sensor that was allowing the light to come back on. But even when you turn the switch off from the wall, *that* switch has a way of turning itself on, too. Perhaps these ghosts don't like the dark and want to have warm light filling the house, or maybe they are going about their daily business and turning the light on so that they can eat dinner, not knowing that they have actually passed on and no longer reside in the living world.

The bathroom sink is yet another of the house's strange quirks that we feel make it paranormal. The water will turn on in the middle of the night. The faucet is tight, verifying that it isn't just vibrating on with passing traffic. That thought process sounds almost more ludicrous than the existence of ghosts in the first place. Mom gets up at all hours of the night to turn it off, only for it to happen again—or if not again that night, another one. These types of events have become so commonplace for my mom that she doesn't even get excited about them any longer. She just gets up and turns off the light or the faucet and returns to bed, going to sleep and not thinking that it is anything overly extraordinary.

There are also noises that emanate from the basement of the house on almost a nightly basis. Banging is heard as though someone is pounding on and the heating vents. There are some nights that it gets to be very loud, and she has to get up, go to the stairs leading to the basement and yell down for the ghosts to keep it quiet and to knock off their racket so that she can get some sleep. Generally, they comply with her wishes, never *completely* stopping, but for the most part taking it down to a dull roar so that she is able to finally drift back into a sound sleep.

On one very special but very odd occasion, Mom had pulled back the covers on her bed only do discover a dried petunia, light purple in color, right in the center of her pillow. She had not changed the sheets on her bed for a couple of days; she had only made the bed in the morning after waking up. She had also had her night clothes on for about two hours prior to going to bed, so it wasn't something that could have fallen off her clothing onto her pillow when she turned down the covers. There is more to this experience though, after discovering the flower and while lying in bed, she felt the lightest touch on her hands. It felt like someone lightly caressing her hands. This happened before she had fallen asleep for the night, so she is absolutely positive that she did not dream the entire incident.

Voices are another common occurrence within the walls of this house. Very often, at differing times of the day and night, she will hear female voices having a discussion. She has a difficult time in pinpointing the location of the voices, but they are definitely coming from within the house. Even though one of the voices is loud and can be heard very easily, it is not a voice that she is able to determine just what is being said. It is most often very muffled.

On one occasion immediately after climbing into bed after an absolutely horrible day, a male voice spoke directly into her ear with a scary, almost evil sounding voice saying, "crabby, crabby, crabby." You see, she had had a very bad day, pretty much the entire day. She is a foster parent in St. Louis County in northeastern Minnesota. She was fostering a newborn baby with a tremendous amount of medical issues, and because my mom is a registered nurse, she was given this child because she required medical attention around the clock. There was a need for feeding tubes and lots of medication to be monitored. It was a stressful situation for her because she is no longer the proverbial spring chicken. When she related this story, she told me that she really was crabby that day. When she finally was able to climb into bed to get a few hours sleep before getting up again to feed this incredibly sick baby, this was when the voice came that really unnerved her—more than any other paranormal event that has occurred in the house to date.

One of the most disturbing occurrences that *I* can remember involved the incident with the lid of her washing machine. As is typical with most houses, the washer and dryer are located in the basement. The basement of this house is seemingly the most active part of the house and never seems to be a disappointment when it comes to paranormal activity. Mom had put her hand on the inside top edge of the washer and bent down to pick up some clothes she wanted to wash when suddenly the washer lid came slamming down on her hand! It hurt like the dickens and she yelled out. I remember her hand being black and blue for over a week.

When she told me this had happened, I came over and decided that I would find a logical explanation for this, because there had never been anything malicious in the house that anyone was aware of. She described the lid's movement as a slam and not that it just fell. There was some velocity when it struck her hand—and it had to be moving down quite hard, judging from the coloration of the bruising on her left hand.

I went to the basement and began to see if I could make this lid fall or slam—either one, on my own hand. I placed my hand on the washer in the same manner that she had and began to bend over as if to pick up clothes with no result. I then began to shake the washer back and forth and side to side trying to make that lid fall—it would have no part of it. I banged and bumped and pushed the washer every which way I could think of to no avail. Finally, I did get the lid to slam down after about ten minutes or so. I hip checked the front of the washer actually lifting the front legs off of the floor, and when the legs contacted the floor again, the lid had some force upon it that threw it closed quite rapidly causing it to slam shut.

The washing machine was a very scary event for my mom, but one of the strangest things that the house has produced thus far is the little boy. A little boy has been seen by several people and described always in the same way. He is about nine or ten years of age with short brown hair. He is wearing a button-down shirt and brown pants. At one point, my mom had been a foster parent of a young boy, and she thought that might be him who had disappeared into her bedroom closet in the middle of the night during one of the sightings. She went to ask him why he was hiding in the closet, but after opening the door, she discovered that there was nobody there. She then went to check on the boy and found him sleeping soundly in his bed.

On another occasion, my wife, Rhonda, saw this very same boy. It was about 3:30 in the morning and she woke from a dead sleep to see him sitting on the second stair from the bottom and off to the side of the stair a little bit. My mom's friend, Bob Nelson, has also seen this little boy lately. He was sleeping one weekend in the guest bedroom, and my youngest son, Jeff, was sleeping in the basement. Bob woke up early in the morning seeing a little boy with dark hair like Jeff walking into Mom's room. He later asked my mom why Jeff was in her room so early in the morning and she replied, "Jeff was never in my room." Jeff had not gotten up early that morning. It was yet another sighting of the little boy. Rhonda feels that he had been punished while still in his physical body by being made to sit on the steps to think about something that he had done wrong.

On October 18, 2006, I decided to set up my two security cameras to see if I would be able to actually capture any paranormal evidence in the house. I set one of the cameras up in the basement pointing toward the stairs and the other one up in the living room directed across the living room and down the hallway toward the bedrooms. I left everything turned on and instructed my mom how to start the VCR recording when she went to bed. She started the recording and then headed off to bed, allowing the cameras to run for six hours each into the middle of the night.

The camera that was located in the upstairs living room ended up not catching anything paranormal at all. The camera in the basement didn't capture anything unusual with the exception of severe interference after only one hour of taping. The recording went to snow on the screen very abruptly. It stayed in a state of static for about twenty seconds at which time the screen began to come back up from the bottom of the frame toward the top and eventually filled back in the entire screen. Then there was a little static that made the VCR I was watching the tape on begin to run its auto tracking, and then the screen returned to normal where it ran flawlessly for a little over five more hours.

I have no explanation for this interference. It definitely had nothing to do with the power going off. If that were to have happened, the digital alarm clock, plugged into the same outlet, would have been flashing, since it doesn't have a battery backup. The camera performed flawlessly up to this point and also performed perfectly after this time. Additionally, this particular camera has not had something like this happen in investigations after this episode, either. It is not proof of the paranormal in any way—I understand that because there could be a rational, mundane explanation for this anomaly, but as yet, I haven't heard one.

Could it be a ghost? Certainly, it could be. Will we ever be certain that a ghost caused it? No. That would be impossible to ever determine. Given all of the activity in the house and all that people who have witnessed things, could it be said that there is a strong possibility of this being caused by a ghost? Of course, a ghost could have caused it. Ghosts mess with electronic equipment probably more often than we actually realize. After all, they are comprised of electromagnetic energy and they need to re-charge their own batteries on a regular basis. This video is available for you to see on our website, and I hope that everyone will take a look at it to try to make a determination for themselves as to whether or not this could be caused by a ghost.

Like I said, I had been in the house on previous occasions to look for ghosts, but in November of 2006, we actually did a full-out team investigation. A few students from Brown Institute who were doing a documentary about ghosts and paranormal investigations for a broadcasting class they were attending, joined the investigation. This was their final project for the class and they were not disappointed. Right off the bat, while setting up cameras, Rhonda made contact with the little boy in the laundry room, and he was witnessed there by several of the group members at that time—including one of the students.

We also had a spirit that kept pacing back and forth from the laundry room to the furnace room in the basement. The psychics decided that this was a separate entity from the one upstairs that Kyle felt was named Allen. He did pick up that Allen was upstairs dressed in work clothes. This sounds strikingly like the description that my grandmother gave of him, which makes me wonder if my grandmother was wrong about it being her father or grandfather but perhaps it was just an older gentleman that appears to look a little bit like him. The name of the little boy has not been determined as yet; I am thinking that we will need to get Christy in the house to finally determine his name, so that perhaps we can do some research on people who have lived in the house formerly.

The results of the investigation were rather disappointing, I must admit. Even though our team goes into an investigation with a neutral attitude regarding whether or not a house is haunted, I was really hoping ahead of time to have found some great evidence. Is it because I am closely tied to this house that I wanted to find the evidence? Of course, it is. I wanted to be able to validate the haunting for my mom, my wife, and me, since we have all had paranormal experiences there regularly for a couple of years after the purchase of the house.

From a professional standpoint, we didn't catch enough evidence to say officially that there is a documented haunting at my mom's house. We will be going back though, or at least I will be for sure. Each time I go back, I will keep secretly hoping that some documentation will be obtained at some point. It is odd *knowing* that ghosts are there. There must be, since there have been so many accounts that have no explanation. I find it a little bit on the frustrating side, too, knowing what is there and not being able to see it in a physical format to prove it—such as still photography, video, or even one EVP.

Chapter Eleven
My Own Rental House

Being a paranormal investigator has been a very interesting obsession for me. It started out with me living in a haunted house back in the early 1990s, where I moved in as a complete skeptic about ghosts and then had a first-hand education on what it was like to see, hear, and feel things that you cannot explain. Here is my story of the house in McGregor, Minnesota.

It was late 1991, and I was currently unemployed and looking for something better in my life. I had applied and took the test to become a corrections officer for the State of Minnesota in a minimum-security prison. This facility was located in an area of the state that I was completely unfamiliar with, Moose Lake. I ended up getting the job and started in early January of the following year. I drove back and forth from Forest Lake, Minnesota to Moose Lake daily—which got very old and tiring very quickly. It was about a two and a half hour drive one-way. I spent almost as much time on the road as I did working, so in a sense, it was very much like working two jobs. I did this self-torture for about a month and a half until I couldn't stand it anymore and finally decided that we (my girlfriend, her son, and I) needed to get very serious about finding some place to flop at night that was perhaps within some reasonable distance to the facility. I needed to function fairly clearly and not just walk through the day like a zombie on auto pilot. The quest for a place to live began.

We looked in Moose Lake and came up short on everything we saw. It was either way too expensive or currently being rented by the families of inmates serving time in the prison. Yes, that seems to be a common practice since the families of these guys don't seem to like the drive all that much, either. Our radius seemed to be growing with each day, and we were actually at the point of hoping for something even halfway, to at least cut down the drive somewhat.

We finally found something. It was a house, but it was something that seemed to come out of the back of some ghost story writer's mind. The hulking old powder blue house stood there in front of us like something we had just seen in an old *B* movie on the late show. It wasn't very inviting at all. Granted, it was during the cold months, and I didn't expect to find trees flourishing in the yard, but it would have been nice to at least have something to look forward to in the spring. Nothing was growing in the yard, and after living there myself, I can understand why.

We walked inside and saw that it wasn't all that bad looking, though it was very old and stale. There were hardwood floors throughout the house without a stitch of carpet in any room, which made walking in the house something that was announced to everyone in the building—well, that and the fact that the floors creaked. The real shocker had to be the dining room, though. It was in between the living room and the kitchen and had no windows of its own. Ambient lighting was all there was for this room, unless you turned on the old light hanging over the table. This wasn't the disturbing part, though. The lighting issues was thoroughly covered by the fact that the room was painted jet black from top to bottom. This black paint seemed to almost suck up every little bit of light that entered the room.

The kitchen itself was really unremarkable and appeared to be normal—well, at least semi-normal. We traversed the old rickety creaking stairs to the floor above to see simply a bathroom and six fairly small bedrooms. All had a door on them for privacy, but most didn't even have any kind of closet to hang up clothes. The price was cheap enough, and we needed to find something before I committed a mass murder from the commute, so we decided to rent the old thing. We moved in. It didn't take a very long time before I realized that this might not have been the best move I had ever made in my life.

I slept pretty well in the old house for a few weeks, but then again, I was so exhausted from all the hours on the road I was putting in to do much else when I was off work. I began to feel a little more like a normal person being able to sleep. Then, after a few weeks, things began to take a little bit of a turn.

I began waking up repeatedly at first and, of course, my logical, skeptical mind didn't think too much of it at the time. I was a little baffled, though. I couldn't really find much of a reason for this waking up other than perhaps since I was no longer in a constant fog, I was thinking more about the daily stresses of being a corrections officer.

Then the noises began to make themselves more prevalent. I would hear a bang and wake up, but would be unable to find out what the cause of the bang was. There were many nights that I got myself out of bed to check to see if the child of the house was awake and playing. It turned out that he was in his bed sleeping soundly. I checked the downstairs and saw nobody inside the house. I checked all the locks on the doors and found nothing out of place.

Then, one night, while going through my checking ritual, I felt it. I felt the eyes staring at me as well as the hairs on the back of my neck standing straight up. I began to get a very uncomfortable feeling inside the house. I even got to the point of giving up the almost nightly ritual of getting up to check the child, downstairs, and doors. In fact, it got to the point where I felt like I was sleeping with one eye open all the time, and, of course, becoming tired at work yet again with the constant fog setting in.

One night while in a surrealistic dream state, by which I mean that I wasn't in a deep sleep and yet I was not awake, I could see a man standing over me on my side of the bed. He was an older man wearing bib overalls. I shot up thinking that someone was finally in the house, and me, being the tough corrections officer, needed to get going full out to stop this intruder. When I got out of bed, the man was suddenly gone. This brought on a whole new wave of feelings from deep inside of me. I felt very cold and confused in a way I'd never felt before, but I told myself that it was all a dream—even though somewhere in the deepest, darkest corners of my mind, I just knew that I was lying to myself in order to keep some semblance of sanity. My skeptical mind could not even entertain the thought of ghosts existing at that moment. These kinds of things were from movies, books, and fairytales and do not really affect anyone in a real-life situation.

One late night, after I had returned home from working an afternoon shift at the prison, the weirdest event I had witnessed to date happened. (Of course, now to think back on this, it seems very mild and even exciting, as I would've loved to have captured this on videotape.) I came home about 11:45 pm and stripped off the brown polyester pants and white cotton shirt that were my uniform and put on some sweatpants and a nice comfortable T-shirt. I made myself a little dinner, as I hadn't eaten anything since long before I'd left. I sat down on the couch that was actually located in the center of the living room due to its shear size; if we didn't place the couch there, we would not have been able to even see our small nineteen-inch television. I turned on a movie on a pay movie channel and began to watch. (Of course, I had to be watching something that was from the horror genre to begin with. This helped to make my experience much more dramatic.)

I had finished eating my dinner and was really getting into the movie when suddenly, I could hear a noise that sounded like water rushing. I turned to my left and could see right through the creepy black dining room to the kitchen sink. To my amazement, the water was on full blast. This faucet was equipped with a lever-type handle that you lift up to get water out of the tap. It was all the way into the up or open position. I mustered up my last little bit of courage and carefully went into the kitchen to see what was going on with the water. When I arrived at the sink, indeed the water was running full open. I then grabbed the handle and pushed it back down into the "off" position with no more water running, not even a drip.

I immediately checked the back door to see if someone had broken into the house, which was a very stupid thing to do. It suddenly hit me that nobody would break into a house in order to turn on the kitchen sink full blast and then run out of the house to go laugh about what they had just done. It about this point that I felt an ice cold chill run down my spine. It started at the base of my skull and ran straight down to the tailbone and then left me. It did not radiate out into any more of my back nor did it run to any extremities.

I was very unnerved now, and decided that I'd had enough horror movies for one night and would head up to bed. Again, I felt the eyes upon me, making every step toward the stairs a chore. I managed to climb to the top of the stairs and decided that I should make sure everything was okay with the child of the house before tucking myself into bed. He was fine, seeming totally oblivious to anything going on in the house.

I could no longer keep this a secret from the girlfriend and we discussed it. To my amazement, she had been feeling many of the same things that I was. Of course, the logical mind wouldn't allow for me to accept the words she was saying, and I heard myself again making excuses for everything saying, "there must be a rational explanation for all of this." I thought that the faucet, being an inanimate object, would be subject to standard, boring old malfunction. Because I worked in a state prison, I had a lot of resources to get my answer to that question. I began to ask several people from the maintenance crew about the faucet to try to determine what was happening with it. I was thinking that the water pressure in the pipes had caused the handle to rise, and once it started, it was going all the way up.

This explanation was shot down by the maintenance guys. These are some of the best maintenance people anywhere, and some had been certified plumbers for over twenty years. When I asked them about my theory, they simply said that this type of thing just couldn't happen. The design of this type of faucet will either perform as it should, or if the seals go, it will shoot out water like I was describing to them—but then you would not be able to shut it off with the handle. You would literally have to turn it off at either the valve, if there is one, or turn it off at the source.

Okay, admittedly I was a little freaked out by this news because my mind could not generate another excuse as to why this could happen. I knew that it was not a result of someone else residing there in the house with me; they were upstairs sleeping and I would have heard the floor creak if someone would have walked past. I knew someone didn't break into the house to turn on the water in the kitchen, and now I knew that the faucet itself could not have been the culprit. I had no logical explanation for what I had witnessed.

It came to pass that we were forced to live with the constant uneasy feeling for several months, and then we found out some very shocking news from the neighbors living around us. They told us that a previous owner of the house had committed suicide in the kitchen of the home by putting a shotgun in his mouth and pulling the trigger. We lived for yet another few months still hearing the noises every night, when going to bed. I literally began to hate bedtime, since it usually meant that I was in for a night of terror.

Eventually, the last straw at the house was reached. The stove in the kitchen decided that, on a whim, it would suddenly catch on fire for no reason. Luckily, it occurred during the day when we were both home and awake, so that we could get the thing unplugged and put the fire out. The fire had melted all of the wiring in the top of the stove as well as down the back of it, rendering it useless from that point on.

The stove incident was the thing that made us want to leave the house as quickly as possible and move into a more normal house. This we were able to do—we got lucky and immediately found another house that we could move into. We moved our beds and clothes first so that we could sleep in the new house and not ever have to spend another scary night amidst the horrible entities that were terrorizing us in the big old blue house in McGregor.

I firmly believe that the worst entity in the house was that of the man that nobody seemed to like or even tried to like, and when he had had enough, he blew his head off with a shotgun. This restless spirit is what did most of the terrorizing in the home, but I would be willing to bet my bottom dollar that there are many more spirits residing within the walls of that old dwelling. I am hoping that some day I can locate the owners of the house and perhaps set up an investigation.

I'd put the paranormal on a back burner for a couple of years, until about 1996, when I was reminiscing about the old blue house while watching a ghost show on television. I then wondered if it may have been a true haunting. I began to research the paranormal at about that time and have been doing it ever since. I, of course, kept it a secret from even the girlfriend that I was looking into this and beginning to study the paranormal, because I didn't want her to think that I was just nuts.

It has been over fourteen years since I'd moved out of that house, but I am fairly sure the ghost of that tormented old man is still residing there. If I ever get to investigate the house, I will be sure to include it in a future writing.

Chapter Twelve
A Wildly Haunted House I Lived In

The house in Chisholm, Minnesota was a real experience and worthy of a chapter here. This was the house that got me to open up about my paranormal research—to actively seek out what causes ghosts to appear to us and why they tend to hang around on the physical plane.

After a number of years doing some small investigations and investigating some cemeteries to see what I could come up with (along with doing more and more research all the time), I moved to Chisholm. I met someone and began a new relationship in this particular house with her. She also had a son who shared the residence with us. The house was pretty normal at first with nothing out of the ordinary happening. My kids from a previous relationship came to me for visitation and would stay in the house. They would tell me of conversations they were having with a little girl who would come into the bedroom at night, and they wondered who she was. We didn't think too much about it, but were becoming more wary since we'd had a couple of occasions where the dogs would get very upset and start growling at blank walls, and even sporadically would run away to hide from some unseen force. Due to the nature of my paranormal research and investigations, I knew that there was at least one ghost in the home, since the puzzle pieces were beginning to fit together. Eventually, circumstances allowed me to gain custody of my children and they came to live with us fulltime in the Chisholm house.

Having the kids at the house began to cause some jealousy and conflict. After all it is very difficult to introduce two more kids into a household that has had an only child for so long—then poof, instant brothers overnight. This situation and others that go along with integrating families provided much conflict and arguing in the household. Conflict is a fantastic ghost kick-starter! That and possibly the small amount of renovation taking place—not really anything noteworthy in the way of changes that I think would anger a ghost into really making its presence known to everyone.

One day my oldest son John came home from school—I believe he was in the fourth grade at the time. He asked if we could have a rat. I was just a wee bit put off by this question, but after finding out that this rat was an albino that the class had been feeding in their room for a project and realizing that he was very friendly, we decided to let him have the rat in our house. We bought the whole tube cage system and it was very nice for the rat. My younger son, Jeff, fell instantly in love with it, too.

I believe, though, that this rat was a great indicator of paranormal activity in the house. It was very strange at times to see him running on his wheel for a very long time, only to jump off and stare out the corner of the cage at something, and then suddenly cower shaking in the corner a few seconds later. He would always act very strangely just before I would get that chill that ran down my spine or before we would have some sort of experience that we could not explain. One night, the rat was acting even more strangely than ever before, and it was a night that I won't soon forget!

We observed our little white rat friend acting strangely and wondered what the big deal was with him. Then we turned in, for what we had hoped would be a good night's sleep. Boy, was I ever wrong! I guess I should stop here for a moment and tell you about the door to the bedroom in which we slept. It was bowed inward, making it difficult to open when latched shut, and when it did open, it was always with a very loud popping sound. Needless to say the younger of the two boys were unable to get this door open when it was shut all the way. I was lying there in bed, sound asleep, when the door suddenly popped open. I was trying to get my heart rate back to normal so I wouldn't have a heart attack, and we wondered how it could have done that. This door had never done this before (and never again afterward).

It was cold outside, and the windows were all shut and nobody had opened an outside door to the house. When I checked, all three boys were sound asleep in their beds and the house was completely dark with nobody else in the house. After many minutes of the two of us trying to figure out just what happened and figuring it to be our ghost, we returned to sleep. I then began to have the weirdest dream that I have ever remembered. I was asleep in our bed, and a ghostly woman, dressed in a long white flowing dress, came floating into the window and hovered very sensually over top of me. Then, in a flash, she turned very evil looking and began to claw at my chest with very long, pointed fingernails. The ghost then began to claw at my legs as she moved down my body. All of a sudden, and in a very quick motion, she would grab my ankles and drag me out of my bed and out the window where I would fall. That is the point where I would always wake up. I say *always wake up* because this was a recurring nightmare that I had time and time again.

On one occasion, while walking up the steps to the bedroom to go to bed, I witnessed an orb actually moving down the steps. This obviously was not a piece of dust being reflected off anything, but a paranormal orb that moved quite deliberately down the stairs. I not only witnessed this once, but on two separate occasions, and both times it appeared exactly the same way, but in different locations on the steps.

Voices were another thing that really got to me at times. I would hear a woman's voice coming from the kitchen while I was in the living room watching television. When I'd heard it originally, I'd turned off the television to see who was speaking. When I heard it again, quite clearly from the kitchen again, saying, "Brian, I don't like you," it was time to actually start investigating much more feverishly. I heard this same female voice several other times while at this house, but I was unable to make out what it was saying—which is the case most of the time when you hear the voice of a ghost, especially with the naked ear.

At this point, I really began to step up the investigation process. I began taping in the basement especially. One particular time, I was taping in the basement and had asked the name of a spirit that I believed was down there. I captured on tape, "Peter, Peter." Of course, I didn't know that I had captured the name at that time. I then backed up from where I was standing, and it felt as though I had backed straight up into a large block of ice. My right shoulder, arm, rear-end, and the upper part of my right leg were freezing. I was also able to see my breath, which was not the case only moments before. It was at this time that I captured the same voice saying that it's name was *Peter*—only now it was saying, "Don't do that again!"

I continued to do EVP in the house for quite some time, getting many that were not very clear, but also getting some answers to my questions. It was a very active house, indeed. At one point in the basement, I actually saw a shadow that moved across the north wall and stood there stationary for what seemed to be about fifteen seconds or so until it finally disappeared. All I can really say about it was that it was wearing a hat.

Unexplainable cold and hot spots were also a very common occurrence in this house. I remember one time, as I was sitting at my computer, which was located in a small alcove off the kitchen, and surfing around on one of my favorite paranormal web sites (ghostvillage.com), suddenly getting extremely hot. This heat was overwhelming! I actually thought that I was going to pass out. I was sweating profusely and felt like I could hardly breathe. (You know that feeling you can get going into an attic or similar location on a hot day with the sun beating down on the roof.) It was not overly warm in the house, and as suddenly as it began, it stopped and everything returned to normal very quickly. This happened to me a couple of different times. My body temperature did not change through the events, though, as I took my temperature on the second occurrence of this phenomenon. My temperature stayed around the normal ninety-eight degrees. It all ended suddenly.

Toward the end of the time that I spent in this house in Chisholm, I began to get sick. Well, at least I thought I was getting sick. I began to not have any energy at all. I felt weak all of the time and nauseated quite often, but never remember really throwing up. I just had that queasy sickly feeling like you might have to be physically sick, but never are. I was tired all the time and seemed to be back into a fog, even though I was sleeping pretty well most nights. The odd thing about it is that when I would leave the house, I would almost instantly feel better. It didn't matter how badly I felt while in the house, it would clear up almost instantly the moment I left the house. It is my very strong belief that the ghosts inside the house were draining their energy off me directly and keeping me feeling this way. When I would leave the house, the energy drain would cease and I would feel much better.

My time in the Chisholm house ended rather abruptly one night when my girlfriend and myself could not see eye to eye on the discipline for the kids and their fighting. I had reached the final straw and my camel was broken in two. I packed up the kids and a few belongings and headed for my mom's house, never to spend another night in this old house. I think that the ghosts in the house manipulated us, making us feel badly and somehow urging us to want to tear at each other's throats, constantly causing the fighting. We started out wonderfully and had a great relationship, but I think that the more time we spent inside the house, the more we drifted apart. It seemed to make have this effect on all who were living there. I don't believe that the house liked me much—probably because I was actively investigating it and there were many times when I would post my findings on the ghost village website. Perhaps this is why the overwhelming heat would hit me when I was on that web site. Perhaps it was some sort of warning.

A psychic friend of ours from California had come to visit us. This trip was planned months before I had left the house. He had planned on spending time with us together but he ended up seeing us separately—part of the time with her and part with me. While he was there, he investigated the house to see what his findings would be. He found there to be seven different spirits living in the house. He ended up doing a cleansing in the house and felt as if they all had left. Since I have not seen my ex-girlfriend in several years, I have not had an opportunity to ask her if the house has remained quiet or not. Perhaps in the darkest corners of the house in Chisholm lurks at lease one of the seven spirits that refuses to leave this house.

The "Peter, Peter" EVP and the "Don't do that again" EVP are available on our website at www.hauntingresearch.com along with several photos taken inside the house.

Epilogue

Over the many years that I have been researching ghosts, I have experienced things that most people never get to experience. I have been in many people's homes trying to help them out; I have stood in cemeteries at three in the morning trying to make contact with spirits and have gone into some fairly well known places, such as Duluth's Depot and the *William A. Irvin*. It is always an adventure, and I recommend paranormal investigation to anyone with the guts to stand in the dark and make contact with spirits on the other side without running away.

Being a paranormal investigator is not something that suits everyone, though. We have had our fair share of people who have wanted to give it a go, going out with our group only to get really freaked out and throw in the towel immediately after. You do have to have a very strong will in order to do this type of work—and if anyone tells you otherwise they are lying to you.

Also, you have to be able to deal with the physical and mental drain that comes along with the territory. When you spend a great deal of time in a haunted location communicating with ghosts, you will get mentally and physically drained over a period of several hours. It is, of course, all dependent on how many spirits there are located at the site you are investigating. One of the most draining for our entire team was the Chase On The Lake Hotel in Walker, Minnesota. That place is loaded with spirits and has so much paranormal activity, it was difficult for our psychics to sort all of it out and make sense of it all. If you are planning on getting into the field of paranormal research, keep in mind that this mental and physical drain will happen to you at some point, so always be prepared to deal with that. If you let it happen, it will wear you down until you feel like you are ready to begin residing on some locked nut ward somewhere.

I also want to make some very strong recommendations to all that wish to venture out by advising that, if at all possible prior to starting a group of investigators, go out with an established group that knows what they are doing. This will help to keep you safer in the field. If you don't have a group in your area that you are able to get to go out with, contact one that you feel can be trusted and ask questions. Ask lots of questions. Get their opinions on how to do things. Most good reputable groups are always willing to help other people who are new to the field to get started.

Consider how to keep the spirits at the location they are investigating. Know the ramifications of not knowing the signs of a possession and how to deal with it. Understand that you need to keep your mental barriers up to a certain extent to not allow just anyone inside of your mind.

Remember, too, that ghosts are just people. They are not evil, nor are they just *Casper the Friendly Ghost*. You see, in all of my research I have been led toward the very simple conclusion and that is that ghosts are just people. They are nothing less and certainly nothing more than that. It has become my belief that ghosts are simply the spirits of people who once lived in a physical body, and once that body died, for whatever reason, their spirits returned back to the realm from which it came. Of course, there are good people and bad people in the world. Thus, it makes sense to follow that thought with the statement that there are good ghosts and bad ghosts.

Just imagine yourself walking down a busy city street and being able to interview everyone that you met along the way. If you were able to do this, you would find out that there are very loving, caring people that would give you the shirt off of their backs and suffer so that you could be warm and comfortable. By the same token though, you will meet people that would take your shirt from your back and laugh at you for being less fortunate than they are. It goes without saying that you would also encounter every differing stage in between both personalities.

There are a lot of people that claim that any negative entity must be a demon. I am sure that there are many of you that will disagree with me, but I have never been able to find any sort of evidence of their existence whatsoever. I have, on the other hand, found plenty of evidence of negative entities that were once human. If you think about it, Jeffrey Dahmer and Ed Gein had spirits inside of them, no matter how twisted and negative those spirits are. These are the types of spirits that exist in a negative haunting and usually are the ones that scare people, even going as far as hurting them physically by scratching, biting or shoving them around. Keep this in mind if you ever decide to conduct paranormal investigations; ghosts were once people, too, and remember that even though they are dead and no longer have a physical body, they deserve our respect.

This even means that we need to be respectful of the places that their spirits dwell. If we visit the old deserted building back in the woods, we must treat that dwelling with respect and not write graffiti on the walls, nor tear anything down or break things. We must also remember that when in a cemetery, the stones are their identities of a time when they were living, so keep in mind that the stones do not get tipped over nor should anything that has been placed in a cemetery be removed. I read an account of someone who was bragging, not too long ago, that they had gone into a cemetery in Washington State and taken a statue of an angel, putting it in the back seat of their car. I was mortified to have read this, and of course, they had made the claims that they were ghost hunters at the time they had done this.

I would also like to discuss something that I hear about on a regular basis: provocation. There are investigators who attempt to get spirits in a location agitated, to get them to show themselves or to show a sign that they are actually there with the investigative team—this is provocation. There are many facets to using this technique that need to be explored by every individual wishing to use them. First and foremost, there is respect. This is something that must be kept in mind at all times, and it must not cross this line. Respect must be maintained—you don't want to get "nasty" with a spirit at any time (especially if the location you are in is someone's home). Keep in mind that these could very easily be family members you are provoking into showing themselves. If you get nasty and loose respect, you could very well have a negative impact on the clients you are trying to help.

The next facet is actual physical danger. It can be dangerous to provoke spirits. They have the ability to scratch, hit, push, and throw things at you. They can also destroy your equipment, so keep all of this in mind if you should decide that you want to use it and cross the respect line. You may get just a little more than you ever bargained for.

The third and final facet I would like to discuss is religious provocation. This one is extremely dangerous, in my opinion. Granted, there are many that will disagree with me on this, but I think that since my experience has been able to bear this out for me, it deserves mentioning here. When religion is introduced into a haunting, nine times out of ten it will make the situation worse than it was before. I have had many clients tell me that they had ghostly activity in the past but when they decided to have the local priest come over and bless their house, it increased in not only the activity level, but in the violence of the haunting itself. It is my belief that since religion and the paranormal are not related in any way, that this should be kept out of it at all times. N.M.P.I. even has people on the team who are religious—and that is okay—but it never is brought into our investigations in way.

Finally, I would like to say "thank you." I want to thank all of the ghosts that have decided to communicate with my team and myself over the years, showing themselves in photographs as well as on videotape. I want to thank all of the people who have taken an interest in our work and have appreciated that fact that we are out there sacrificing ourselves mentally and physically to bring information out to the public so that we can show what actually does happen to us beyond this physical, living world we all know and love.

Paranormal Glossary of Terminology

This glossary of paranormal terms is spelled out in my own words. These are terms that have been around for a very long time and widely used in paranormal circles. To agree or disagree with the terms is strictly up to you. Many of them have been interpreted differently over the years and not everyone agrees on every term and its meaning. This is the paradox that is the paranormal world.

Age Regression

This is a process by which we travel back to a stage in our lives when we were younger. This is done through hypnosis.

Akashic Record

This is a fabled document. A contract per se that records a person's past, present, and future lives as well as any parallel lives.

Analog Media

This describes any media that is used for collection of paranormal evidence that is not digital in nature.

Apparition

This is the actual visual appearance of any spirit or ghost, by whichever name you choose to call them, that doesn't necessarily take the shape of a human form. This form may or may not show intelligence.

Astral Projection

This is the technique of projecting one's consciousness into the spirit world. It is rumored that this can be most easily done during sleep. It is believed by some that the sudden "jerk" that one gets when just asleep and then awakened suddenly is the consciousness returning back into our bodies very quickly. It is also stated that dreams are a form of astral projection.

Automatic Writing

This is a method of communication with the spirit world. It involves the use of a normal writing utensil and paper. It involves someone holding the writing utensil and allowing a spirit to take control of their body. During this time, other people ask questions of the spirit in hopes that the spirit will write the answer on the paper through the person they have taken over.

Autonographist

This is a person who is a professional automatic writer. These people usually travel around performing this for people that wish to contact a loved one.

Channeler

This is a person who is able to make direct contact with a spirit and allow it to take over his or her body. The surrounding people can then ask whatever questions they would like of the spirit to hopefully get some answers.

Channeling Board

This is a board that is used for communication with spirits. Also known as a "Ouija" board or talking board. This is a very misunderstood tool that comes equipped with multiples of legends and rumors. When it is used, the users allow the spirits being contacted to use their bodies, very much like the channeler does. This is a very large contributing factor to people's misconception of the board. Many feel that they are inherently evil because there have been accounts throughout the history of this tool that have been very negative. People that allow spirits to enter their bodies usually cause the negative aspect when they do not tell them to leave prior to putting the board away. They allow these entities to remain in our world and this can cause a serious problem if this spirit is negative in nature.

(Please note that *Ouija* is a registered trademark of Parker Brother's Games.)

Clairalience

This is the ability to use smell to receive a spirit's message. Things like perfume, cigarette, or cigar smoke are among the most predominant smells noted throughout history.

Clairambience

This is the ability to use taste to receive a spirit's message. Generally, it is not an exact taste but more of a general sweet, sour, etc.

Clairaudience

This is the ability to use sound to receive a spirit's message. Many times people will hear their names whispered in their ears or may even have entire conversations with a spirit, which can be very useful in gathering information on an investigation.

Clairsentience

This is the ability to use feeling or sensations to receive a spirit's message. I have this ability as I get a chill that runs down my spine from the base of the skull to the tailbone that feels like a small sharp electrical charge. It differs from individual to individual.

Clairvoyance

This is the ability to use sight to receive a spirits' messages. There have been many accounts throughout history of people being able to see spirits. Our team has a couple of people on it with this ability and it is an invaluable tool for investigations.

Class A EVP

This is the absolute best classification of EVP. It is one that comes directly off of the tape and is very clearly understood by almost everyone who hears it. It requires no filtering or stretching in order to be heard and understood.

Class B EVP

This is the second best classification of EVP. It is sometimes slightly difficult to understand directly from the tape and requires some amount of filtering and/or stretching in order to be heard and understood. This classification also results in some dispute over exactly what is being said on the EVP, and some debate will often occur. There will, however, be a majority of people listening to it that will agree on what is being stated.

Class C EVP

This classification is the worst EVP that can be recorded. It is very difficult to understand and is seldom agreed upon as to what is being said. This recording is such that you know something is there, but directly from the tape, it cannot be discerned in any way as to what it is actually being said. It requires an extreme amount of filtering and stretching to even come close to understanding the sounds recorded. These recordings do serve a purpose to the investigator, however. They can at least give some semblance of definition to the questions asked upon a return investigation. You may be able to get a name or date that may help you in the future, but they offer no real proof to the general public of the paranormal.

Collective Apparition

This is an apparition that is seen by many witnesses at the same time. Even though it has been notated several times throughout history, it is indeed a very rare occurrence.

Digital Media

This is a term that refers to media used for collecting audio, photographic, and video evidence of spirits. It uses a series of ones and zeros to store this information for a computer instead of using tape or negative.

Discarnate

This is a actually a very old term. The meaning is that of a spirit that has no actual body or form. This would be the case of any spirit that has not manifested into an apparition or shadow.

Ectoplasm

This is a residue that is left behind by a spirit. When you have seen evidence of an ectoplasm or "ecto," you have actually just missed the ghost itself and only captured the momentary trail left behind by its presence.

Electronic Voice Phenomena or EVP

These are voices of spirits. They are recorded onto a recording media such as audiotape or even videotape. The new wave of recording is on digital voice recorders or DVR. This method is not without flaw, as it has issue with what is known as archival noise and also leaves you with no "hard" evidence to back up any claims of the paranormal. There are classifications of EVP with "Class C" being the lowest grade of recording that can barely be understood if at all. The next higher classification is that of "Class B" EVP. This classification is usually easily heard to be there and recognized as a ghost's voice, but most that hear it will hear it say different things and will quite often debate what is said quite extensively. The highest classification of EVP is the "Class A" EVP. This one is quite clearly understood even in its raw form and doesn't require any cleaning or filtering to be understood as saying one thing by nearly all that hear it. These phenomena aren't necessarily, if ever heard by the human ear itself. These voices of the dead are usually out of the human ear's hearing range but not out of the range of the recording microphone.

Entity

This term is another that is used to describe a ghost. This term is generally looked at as being an evil presence by most, though, or a negative haunting. The term is also something that is used by many who believe in demons and is used to describe them in some of these negative or evil hauntings.

Extrasensory Perception or ESP

This is an awareness of outside happenings or information that is obtained through any senses other than the normal human senses.

Ghost

This is a spirit, soul, or life force that has left the human body to reside in the spirit world. It can be a visual manifestation in the form of orb, shadow, or apparition, but it doesn't have to be visual at all. It can come and go from the spirit world to our own world at will and for any reason. A ghost can be interactive or residual in nature.

Ghost Buster

This term is a technical one in nature. It refers to either a ghost hunter or paranormal investigator who is able to rid the area of spirits and keep them away.

Ghost Hunter

This is an individual who usually gets together with some friends to explore cemeteries or other reportedly haunted locations, primarily for the thrill of the "hunt." They are more the weekend hobbyists looking for a fun evening with some friends. They, generally, are using digital equipment and are not overly concerned with stable verifiable evidence nor are they astute at reviewing the evidence that they do collect.

Hypnotherapy

This is a method of treating ailments through the use of hypnosis.

Interactive Haunting

This is a situation where a ghost is showing obvious consciousness. They are able to answer pertinent questions, be knowledgeable of current events, know the names of the witnesses at the scene of the haunting, etc. They don't necessarily have to be interacting from within our own world. They can use voice from their world, which is why we get garbled messages and even backwards EVP at times.

Matrixing

This condition refers to the human brain looking at patterns in photographs and trying to find familiarities in that pattern. Whether that pattern be tree bark, leaves, and branches, etc. The human mind is always trying to find familiarity where there is chaos. This is the condition that is present when people see faces in wood grain or wallpaper, etc. It is also the condition that we use when we see tanks and battleships in the clouds floating overhead.

Medium

This is a person who possesses a special gift and can act as a bridge between the living and the spirit world. This is the most common type of "psychic" ability there is.

Metaphysics

This is a field of study that is dedicated to the nature of reality; an underlying, philosophical, or theoretical principle.

Motion Blur

This is the effect of moving a camera before the photograph is finished being taken. This happens most frequently with digital cameras. Due to nearly silent operation, it is not always easily recognized when the photo is finished recording. If the camera is moved during this period you will get varying degrees of blur within the photograph. This is not due to paranormal activity, and any photograph with this blur should be deleted and not considered evidence of the paranormal in any way.

Mundane

This term describes a condition of dust, pollen, or some other occurrence which may be confused as paranormal in nature when reviewing evidence collected during a paranormal investigation.

Negative Entity

This is the bad ghost. This is the spirit of someone who was not a good person while alive. These are the serial murders, rapists, and thieves that inhabit our world. When our bodies die, this negative spirit moves to the spirit world and is just as bad as a ghost as when living, since this spirit is what made the person who he/she was in life to begin with.

Orbs

Orbs are ghosts. Since they are electromagnetic energy, the orb is the most natural relaxed state of a ghost. It is the basic building block that apparitions and shadows are made of. They take on extra energy to form into other forms. Generally when filmed, they appear very solid and three dimensional, where as dust films very light and transparent, usually with a ring around it (but the ring isn't required for an orb to be dust). Only about one percent of orbs captured on still photography these days are paranormal in nature.

Other Side

This is a term used to describe the spirit world, the place that spirits go after the body dies on the physical plane.

Paranormal

This is a term used to describe unusual activity. When the word is dissected, it directly means "above normal" or "outside of normal." It generally involves apparitions, spirits, hauntings, monsters, etc. This term defines anything for which there is no scientific explanation.

Parapsychology

This is the study of phenomena whether it is real or supposed. These phenomena appear to have no explanation currently accepted by the scientific world.

Paranormal Investigator

This is the term used to describe the professional. This is the person who puts evidence collection and integrity of that evidence in the forefront. This investigator is in control of his/her environment in which evidence is collected, so as to know where everyone is located. The paranormal investigator takes great care in setting up equipment and photographic shots, and also takes great care to avoid shiny highly reflective surfaces wherever possible, in the attempt to eliminate the possibility of mundane captures.

Past-Life-Regression

This is the use of hypnosis in order to bring someone back to a former life lived. This is done in a trance-like state.

Phenomenon

This is an inexplicable fact or occurrence that is unusual or profound.

Physical Mediumship

This is a term that is not very widely used anymore, but it means that a medium is communicating with spirits by using both physical energies as well as the consciousness of the medium.

Place Memories

This term refers to any location that captures energy and then later uses it to record an image of an event that happened in the past and then later replays that event.

Planchette

This is the pointing device that is used with a channeling or "Ouija" board. It doesn't necessarily have to be a special device as an inverted glass is sometimes used in its place.

Poltergeist

This term is German, which literally translated means "noisy ghost." This is a phenomenon is usually experienced more often than it is seen, and is more descriptive of a type of haunting occurring in a location. The poltergeist is very interactive with the environment and lets the living know it is there, generally by making noise and moving objects at the location.

Progression Hypnotherapy

This is a term that constitutes the visitation of future lives by the use of hypnosis.

PSI

This term is used as a blanket to describe all psychic ability.

Psychic

This is a term used to describe any person who is able to tap into nonphysical forces through empathetic feeling.

Psychokinesis

This is a term that describes anyone with the ability to use their mind to move objects.

Psychosomatics

This term describes a field of study that states that the medical health of a person's body is directly related to that person's mind and emotions. This relates to the paranormal in that, many times throughout history, people have claimed that ghosts have made them sick or injured.

Reincarnation

This is the theory that a spirit leaves a body that it had inhabited upon death. This spirit will reside in the spirit world for an undetermined amount of time, will then cross over into the light and be immediately re-born into another living body at birth.

Residual Haunting

This is a haunting that is not interactive with its environment. It is an impression that has been left on a particular area and is replayed over and over. This has been equated to playing a video, rewinding it and playing it again.

Shadow

This is another form of ghost. They can manifest in many different ways and appearing as a dark, non-descript shadow is just another way that they can make their presence known.

Sixth Sense

This term is used to describe anyone with psychic abilities.

Soul Loss

This is yet another old term that is not used very often today. It means that there is a loss of vital energy that occurs when there is a trauma of some sort to the physical, mental, or emotions of the human spirit.

Spirit

This is another term for a ghost. Some will argue that this is a ghost prior to leaving the human body upon death. It is an electromagnetic energy that is also referred to by some as a soul—the little voice that we hear in the back of our minds. It makes us who we are, whether it be a good person or a bad one. This is the essence of our being, and without it, we are merely an empty shell.

Spirit Communicator

Although rarely if ever used these days, this term has the meaning of a spirit that uses a medium to communicate with the living, whether that be verbally or visually.

Spirit Operator

This term refers to a spirit that physically manipulates something through the use of a medium.

Spirit World

This is the place that a spirit would return to after the death of the body it has inhabited. This is another plane of existence that interacts very often with our own world of the living.

Spirit Guide

This is the spirit of a once-living human being that has chosen to remain in contact with us living people for any reason. Because each one of us has a spirit within us, this spirit guide contacts that spirit within us and provides direction and sometimes keeps us out of harms way. I believe that this comes across in the form of our conscience or that little gut feeling that tells us we are making an unwise decision.

Superpersonalities

This is a term that is used to describe negative entities but is not widely used.

Telepathy

This term describes communicating through the use of the mind as opposed to using the other natural human senses.

Trance Mediumship

This old term is fairly obscure, not readily used anymore. It is a term that describes a sharing of energy between a spirit and a medium through the use of a trance.

Vortex

This term is used to describe a residual effect of what is left when a spirit moves from the spirit world to our own. It can appear and last for extended periods of time. It has been noticed that paranormal activity has increased after these phenomena have been witnessed on film. It does resemble the ectoplasm in some forms but can last much longer and may also have a "swirling" appearance.

Afterward
Getting to Know The Paranormal Investigator Brian Leffler

Brian Leffler lives in the quiet, well, semi-quiet town of Kee-watin, Minnesota with his wife, Rhonda, and two boys, John and Jeff.

He enjoys scuba diving and being in Minnesota with its over ten thousand lakes, giving him plenty of opportunity to be under water on a fairly regular basis! A member of the Itasca County Sheriff's Department dive team, Brian has served on this team with a great group of people and has found that this is one way for him to give something back to the community—something that most people are not able to give. He dedicates a lot of time training under water so that when there is someone who has lost a loved one by drowning, he and the team can go retrieve the remains for the family. It does sound like a gruesome affair, but it is a necessary job that is very much appreciated by the community, and especially the unfortunate families of the lost individual. It gives a lot of satisfaction to bring someone home to their family so that they can have a proper burial and memorial service, and can be laid to rest with the respect and dignity that they deserve.

Brian is also a gunsmith with his own business called Range Gun Works. He finds that he provides another service to people as hunting and shooting are very big events on the Iron Range in northern Minnesota.

Researching ghostly activity for over ten years now, he has built quite a reputation for having ideas about the paranormal that don't fit directly with everyone else's ideas. He strives to be different and original, taking what other researchers before him have developed and building on their ideas, and then progressing forward. Brian believes that just because the wheel was invented, doesn't mean that there isn't room for improvements to be made.

Having many different ideas about the ghosts than other subscribers, his theories are quite sound—and he has even been able to prove some of them—specifically orb activity, which will be discussed in depth further along. The discovery of this now proven theory has been one of the most exciting moments in all of his, or his team's endeavors so far. Pursuing the unexplained vigorously, Brian looks forward to proving other theories as he and his team follow ghosts over the coming years.

Rhonda Leffler, Brian's wife, makes up the stable backbone for the lives of the Leffler family. Through personal turmoil over the years, she has maintained a steady and strong resolve that has been the very strong glue for the family. If it were not for her, this book would never have been written because Brian would not have been able to bring all of this information together. She is an integral part of the Northern Minnesota Paranormal Investigators, both on investigations and when she steps back to stay with the boys or work instead of attending an investigation. She is helping in more ways than just attending investigations and using her psychic abilities to help provide that road map for the team to follow during an investigation, thereby helping them get some of the fantastic results over the years.

Rhonda does much more than just investigate ghosts; she provides a semblance of organization. She stays home to do other things that need to be done to keep the household afloat in the real world and keeps Brian going from day to day—and he thanks her for every moment that she exists in his life.

The boys, John and Jeff, are just pretty normal kids who have been through a lot in their lives. They are getting better though and both believe that ghosts exist. John has stated that he wants very much to carry on the family tradition of chasing ghosts, but it is nice that neither boy is afraid of the existence of the paranormal. When John and Jeff each reach the age of eighteen, Brian hopes that they will want to follow in his footsteps and perhaps they will be the ones to provide the absolute proof of the other side.